396 HOURS

—A COLLECTION OF STORIES—

EDITORS-IN-CHIEF
Sam Bilheimer
Meredith Raiford
Phillip Wentirine

ADDITIONAL EDITING
Krystal Davidowitz
Caroline Fraley
Raptor Grant
Jacob Harn
Pamela Hnyla
Miguel Mendoza
Heather Peters
Nicole Sundstrom
Carl Rosen

BOOK LAYOUT
Sam Bilheimer, with thanks to Susan Bilheimer

COVER DESIGN
Ryan Huffman
thewhitebull.com

Copyright © 2013 Thin Cat Press

ISBN: 1482793954
ISBN-13: 978-1482793956

For our friends, families, and cats, thin or fat, everywhere.

CONTENTS

INTRODUCTION

There's nothing greater than to be inspired. All that makes life a glorious endeavor derives from that. Love in its transient or perennial bloom, the letting go of all restraint in the service of the heart's reach, the making of things that fly. Something blows on the coals of imagination, and we have our moments on fire. It wants to move through us. We know it does. Into the world and onto the air in machines that come from our fingertips. Apparently it only takes 396 hours. All we have to do is stretch ourselves, breathe in, and have the guts to put out our hands.

Sometimes it's something outside us that causes it. A story, a poem, a painting, a strain of music, the color of light in a certain place, or the angle of it when it strikes water or snow or sand or skin, a sudden breadth of wildflowers, the shudder of memory tripped in the mouth, the curve of a hip, a ferocious beauty or a tender one, a lick of comic salt, a trick of bourbon. The stories in this book smolder with peculiar things. I could feel the ruddy heat of them in the room when these writers gathered. It took nothing to let the air in. A suggestion. That's all.

So they made this book. From scratch. Edited it. Encouraged each other, and there are few better things artists can do. Layout, design, aerodynamics, everything. To publish themselves. Not because going indie is fashionable, but because it's possible. Not to set themselves alongside Walt Whitman, Virginia Woolf, Anaïs Nin, and the like, but to lock arms in a singular endeavor. Not to prove the connection between literary legitimacy and traditional publishing is crumbling—we all know self-published books are now reviewed in the *New York Times* and *Publishers Weekly*, and every day more established authors are going out on their own—but because they believe in the work and want to share it. Each one of them does.

I get it. I really do. When you love the work, you want to see who you are when you put yourself in a place where you can call yourself by it. And if you build a kite, there is this wonderful feeling that attends when you sail it yourself. It's like a voice that way. One doesn't need anyone to tell you it's worth raising. One only needs the wind and the will and the capacity for joy in loosing the machine that has come out of you. If it's yar, folks will see it as it should be seen. Soaring.

The authors here are inspired and inspiring. This is a marvelous book of dreams.

Mark Ari
March, 2013

FICTION

VILLAGE INN
Hurley Winkler

The chessboard sat there on weeknights, surrounded by coffee and cigarettes, terrible pie and teenaged boys. The boys would leave home for the night, unannounced to their mothers. They'd tag the train cars and later join together at the Village Inn to play chess. Occasionally, an elderly man who had just lost his wife or a straggler who'd taken up the bottle again would stand aside and watch. These men would remember their grandfathers, who'd taught them the rules of this very game.

Past dawn, the boys would move down Third Street to the only high school in town. They'd take out a pencil and few sheets of paper to draw graffiti ideas for the late night ahead. A teacher doodled equations on a chalkboard, no longer asking the boys to pay attention. No one said a word about the smells of stale coffee and cigarettes dragged in from the Inn.

Some nights the old men would join the boys, competing in a game of chess or two. A filled paper bag sat next to the town drunk as he peered over the board at his opponents, eyes glazed over. The boys never took a drop from that bag.

The mothers never came into the boys' bedrooms to check at night, never alarmed to see sheets emptied of sons.

The latest school picture stuck to the refrigerator, replaced by the next each fall.

THE PORTRAIT ON THE WALL
Miguel Mendoza

anti psychotic

The doctors had said chlorpromazine was a friend, but in the kitchen, the portrait of his mother often advised him not to take it. And who was he to go against the wishes of his mother, *ough...* who kept a careful eye on him from her frame? Anton *uh ho* Lukov always respected his mother. To disobey one's mother, as she often told him, was to condemn oneself to a life of eternal suffering. *yeah oh. bad.*

Because of this, he chose to eat in his room, away from the critical gaze of his mother. She always had something to say about his manners. In his room, he could eat relatively undisturbed, though sometimes he would be visited by The Bearded Man, who had a thing for climbing furniture and was particularly fond of dancing in the nude. But The Bearded Man was far better company than his own mother, Anton had to admit. Sometimes, Anton would play games with The Bearded Man. They would play tag, or hide and seek; The Bearded Man would always win. And when the children came to visit, the games were even more fun. Of course, the shelter of his room would only provide a few hours of rest, because if his mother was left alone for more than a while, she would wail and scream, and Anton would hear this even in his room with the door shut. *poor Anton ...*

"You are a horrible son," she would say. "You leave your old mother alone to die." But sometimes she'd be sweet and say, "Won't you come spend some time with your mother, little Anton?" Anton knew better than to refuse her, for if he did the insults his mother would spew dug deep at his heart. "You idiot! How I wish you'd been a girl, you already look like one anyway," his mother would declare. "Soap your mouth, you brute! Show some respect." And she would not stop screaming and yelling until he did.

manipulative

During the evenings, Anton liked to watch TV. Despite his greying hair, he'd watch cartoons—cartoons depicting rabbits were his favorite—and would laugh hysterically when something funny happened. His mother, of course, saw fault in this and would scream for him to turn the TV off immediately. Anton, feeling rebellious, sometimes ignored her, and turned the volume up, but then his mother would wail louder and louder, competing with the TV, until Anton, defeated, would finally turn it off. If this happened Anton would be too upset to talk to The Bearded Man, or the children, so he would just sit there and pluck out little strands of hair, one by one, until a new little bald spot formed on the side of his head. Then he'd get up and sit in his dark room.

liar

poor man this ...

Anton's sister would check on him sometimes, when she was not busy with her children and her husband. She'd bring cookies. She'd also bring chlorpromazine. When this happened, Anton had clear instructions from his mother. She always kept count of the pills he should have taken, and would say, "Nine," or, "Twelve," and Anton would know how many to flush down the toilet. His mother would also instruct him to comb his hair very carefully so that none of his small bald spots showed. Anton's sister never looked very closely. *god this poor man...*

Anton's mother never talked to his sister, but once she left, his mother would say, "Look, look Anton. *She* knows how to please her mother. *She* is a good child, not like you, you mindless cretin." Other times, she would simply say, "Oh, Anton look. Look how grown my baby girl is." But whatever sweetness his mother could obtain from his sister's visit, it would disappear almost as soon as she closed the door. Then it was back to, "Anton, the frame is crooked. Have you no eyes?" And "Anton, won't you be a good son and dust your mother's frame?"

—

Please sir, get down from there," Anton begged. The Bearded Man had once more climbed atop an old dresser. "If my mother sees you, it will be the end of me." *take his advice*

"Fool," said The Bearded Man, "your mother is dead. Climb up here with me and enjoy the view." Anton placed a chair next to the dresser, attempting to bring The Bearded Man down.

very cool. "For the love of God, put some clothes on."

"*Never.* I happen to enjoy the breeze on my genitalia. Unbind yourself, my good man, and experience the freedom to which a man is entitled!"

"The children," said Anton, "the children will see you."

"The children are playing outside. Perhaps you ought to join them?"

"I can't. If my mother saw—"

"Fool," the Bearded Man interrupted. "Your mother is dead. *Dead*. Knock a couple pills down and see for yourself." This suggestion had an ill effect on Anton. He knew very well that his mother did not like him taking his medicine. He went to his room and opened the drawer where he kept the medicine. He unscrewed the cap. But before he could place a pill in his mouth, a boy came running into the room. The boy was shouting, "Hide me, hide me!"

agh!

"Please, hush. If my mother hears you..."

"Ooo, can I have one, mister?"

take your medicine!

"These are mine, I can't give you any."

"Please, mister?"

"I can't."

"If you don't, I'll go tell your mother you're taking medicine," the boy threatened. Anton saw no alternative but to give the boy what he wanted, and so he said, "Just one."

But as he was handing the boy the pill, the boy snatched the bottle from Anton's hands and spilled all the little pills everywhere.

"Damn." The boy took off running, with no pills at all. Then Anton heard the terrifying voice of his mother. *she is so mean*

"Who are you talking to, you walking imbecile?" she asked. Anton ran to the bathroom to hide, but inside he knew it was no use. "I want you in my sight in five seconds, you babbling dolt." Anton locked the door. She was hanging on the wall, what could she do?

"One..." she said. Anton covered his ears, but he realized he could still hear her.

"Two…" Anton was drooling now, banging his head on the door, trying to get his mother to shut up.

"Three…" Anton unlocked the door. He had to go. He had to. *this is so sad; what a cruel.*

"Four…" Anton ran to the kitchen. He saw there *thing* the portrait of his mother. Anton closed his eyes. He put his trembling hands over his eyes.

"Five," she said. Anton heard nothing for a second, then an increasingly loud noise. It was an intermittent pulse; he heard it and felt it inside his ears, inside his head. The droning sound convulsed him and filled his heart with fear. It was a primeval sound, the sound of his conception, perhaps. It felt alive and organic. It was irregular, but somehow consistent. The noise undulated and terrorized him. Anton crawled out of the kitchen, not wanting to look back at the portrait of his mother. He crawled to his room, still with the horrifying noise in his head.

heart beat

Anton Lukov brought the blankets to his neck. The noise had subsided, but the darkness intensified his panic. He saw in the darkness all manner of things. Rats ate a baby alive in one corner of the room, while a snake gorged on the carcass of some furry animal in another corner. Anton felt himself sweating beneath the blankets, but he didn't care. He tried closing his eyes, but every time he did, he pictured images of terror and destruction. A blade sunk into a woman's cheek. Grotesque and lascivious faces leered at him from the darkness of his room. An old woman smiled at him, and her teeth were putrid with decay. He closed his eyes; he opened them, but found no relief within either darkness.

actively hallucinating

Later, he heard the squeals of several creatures, and a cacophony of voices shouting and shrieking distantly, arguing about some unknown matter. But above all this discordance, he heard the soft harmony of crickets chirping outside his window. Anton tried to concentrate on this sound to block from his mind the shrieks that were plaguing the house. In the background of the crickets' stridulation, he heard the wailing of his mother. But Anton soon discovered that the chirping, too, made him uneasy. He began feeling itchy underneath his blankets. His scalp itched madly. He scratched. Anton felt the crawling of insects on his legs, multiple little legs wiggling all over his body. He pulled the blankets off and found several insects on his bed. An ugly woman with stars tattooed to her eyelids grinned and said, "For good luck, dear." *ah scary!*

Something was going on outside Anton's room; every minute another stranger entered. Two little girls entered and sat on his insect-filled bed. The noise would not subside. The crickets got louder and louder. Eventually, Anton discovered that he understood them. The damned crickets seemed to be talking to him.

"Your mother is waiting for you," they said.

"The idiot son won't go to his mother," one exclaimed. *jesus christ*

Another said, "He deserves to die."

A particularly malevolent voice said, "We'll eat him while he sleeps."

And the crickets kept their barrage of insults and mockery throughout the night. The vile insects were about as bad as Anton's mother.

"Grow a pair and tell your mommy off," one said. Anton thought of going outside and stomping on the grass in the hope of killing some of the loud-mouthed bastards. But then he had a better idea. Anton opened the window in his room and slipped outside, barefoot as he was. He walked around to the garage and got a *ohno...*

can of gasoline. Anton smiled. He couldn't help but drool a little. The bastards would pay. He unscrewed the cap and tossed it aside. Then he began emptying the container out on the grass. It felt good. He felt empowered. Anton did not stop until the whole can was empty.

Before Anton could light the fire, however, he saw The Bearded Man out in the middle of the street, dancing a lovely waltz.

"Isn't it a bit late to be starting blazes, my good man?" asked the Bearded Man. *he is meant...*

Anton looked at him stupefied. He bit and gnawed at his fingernails. He ran his hand through his patchy hair and said, "They might see you naked."

"But everyone's asleep, sir."

"Yes, but they will awake when I light these bastards."

"What bastards?"

"The crickets, they won't shut up."

"Have you tried asking nicely?" asked the Bearded Man.

"No, these bastards won't listen to reason. Fire is the only way."

"I see. But sir, you need firewood to start a fire."

"No, the grass will burn nicely."

"It won't last without wood. Perhaps the frame of an old portrait?" *So Good!*

Anton considered the prospect. Firewood *would* make the fire last longer. A longer fire meant more dead bastards. But his mother would not take kindly. She loved her portrait, hanging there on the wall. Anton jumped back into his room. There was a group of boys sitting on his bed now, talking about their nephews and grandsons, although the boys in the group were no older than seven. An old man nearby was cleaning his teeth with something shiny. The chair in Anton's bedroom was occupied by a couple, who rocked indecently and waved their arms in the air. Ladies in long dresses copulated with men wearing cummerbunds; the trill of their hushed voices resonated conspicuously, but Anton didn't care. He snuck into the kitchen, where the portrait of his mother hung, as ever, on the wall.

"Little Anton, what are you doing out of your room?" she asked. *hell yes!*

"I don't want to talk to you anymore." Anton closed his eyes. "I want to take my medicine." The house went quiet.

All the strangers stopped what they were doing and turned to stare at Anton. Even the children couldn't believe what they had heard.

"Anton, you silly boy, go to your room, and I will bring you a nice potato soup," said his mother. Anton feared the feigned sweetness in his mother's voice. He already had the matchbox in his pocket. *do it!*

But as Anton reached for the portrait, he found himself for the first time really looking at it. And he saw his mother. Her hair was wild and her eyes were stern and menacing. The many lines on her face marked her tensions and her struggles. Anton dared to think that perhaps once, his mother had been beautiful. But staring at her portrait, all he saw were the vestiges of a once-happy woman. The residue of what once had been a delightful lady, young and spirited, and ready to give everything of herself at a moment's notice—for him. This was the way she had been when alive. The portrait would never do his mother justice. Her cerulean eyes were washed away by encroaching sepia. Now Anton's wonderful memories of her were overpowered by a horrible portrait of his mother at her worst. He thought of the way she kept from smiling because she was embarrassed to show her ruined teeth. The portrait only showed an embittered old woman, but it did not show her as she was or as Anton wished to remember her.

Anton found himself unable to fear her. She was no longer a tyrant, but a sad and bitter woman, seeking release. Anton had to release her. He tore the portrait from the wall and flung the front door open. He tossed the horrible portrait of his mother on the ground and struck a match. He let the match drop, and as it hit the grass, the whole ground erupted in flames. The brightness and the heat overwhelmed Anton. He saw the portrait of his mother burning. The sight brought relief. The horrible monster burned, and so did the countless crickets that disheartened him. Anton felt himself a god with unlimited power. He danced and sang in joy and excitement.

"Bravo. Bravo!" screamed The Bearded Man. "I congratulate you, my friend, you are a free man. However, there is one more thing to do."

"And what's that?" asked Anton.

The Bearded Man danced a fabulous hokey pokey as he said, "Your medicine, my good man." Anton understood. The flames now engulfed almost the whole of the yard. Worse still, the fire made the front door impassable. But Anton remembered the window. He ran. It was his only chance. Anton easily climbed inside through the window. His room danced with the flickering fire. There were people there too, all staring at Anton without saying a word. But Anton no longer concerned himself with his strange visitors. He fell to the floor and ran his hands all over the carpet, trying to find the medicine that the one brat had odiously spilled all over the floor. He found many to be crushed, but some were not. Those he found intact, he popped in his mouth. *oh god he's gonna brrr!*

Satisfied, Anton crashed into his bed and stared at the popcorn on his ceiling. He found eerie figures but managed to concentrate on one that looked like a rabbit. And so Anton stared at this rabbit on his ceiling while the flames outside illuminated his bedroom. It was not long, however, before the wailing of a siren broke his concentration, and although he tried with all his might, he couldn't find the rabbit again. Anton looked up to find his room empty; the people in his room were all gone except for The Bearded Man, who had climbed on top of his desk and was sitting there quite naked. Anton smiled and waved at The Bearded Man, and The Bearded Man smiled and waved back. *aww*

The sirens grew louder still, and outside, Anton heard the voices of his neighbors, all shouting in unison like madmen. But Anton didn't care and a strange calm overtook him. He found the rabbit on the ceiling again. Anton tried hard to look for little baby rabbits among the popcorn of his ceiling because he figured the rabbit might be lonely. But Anton never found the baby rabbits because he heard someone banging on his door. "The firemen are here," Anton said to The Bearded Man, but when Anton turned, he saw The Bearded Man had gone.

wow, very cool narration!

[handwritten annotations: "one of the rivers in Hell that made you forget your problems"; "greek spirit of forget-fulness ?"; "I have a horrible memory! so yes"; "what's so special"]

IN TRANSIT: LETHE
Sam Bilheimer

Y ou know that feeling when you <u>forget</u>
something? When all you remember is
forgetting it, and trying to remember it just
makes everything around you go blurry and concave-
y like a squeezed aluminum can? I'm trying to
remember something in particular when I find myself
walking down an alleyway, sleepy grey all along the
brick walls. I come across a box, ribboned and
wrapped with violet cloth. I try to open it but notice a
brass keyhole <u>shaped like a mouth.</u> Suddenly, I
remember dancing someplace very familiar, but at the
same time, I'm forgetting.

So I wait, cradled in the corner with the violet box
until one day, I think I remember what it was I'd
forgotten all that time ago. I start to write, using the
pen I've kept in my pocket for just this occasion and
the side of the violet box as paper because it's the only
thing in the alleyway with me. But the blue ink from

the pen blends in with the violet on the box, and I get frustrated.

And so I bang my fists on the ground, <u>bloodying my knuckles</u>. *jeeze dude*

And so I scream for anyone to bring me something to write on to remember what I'd forgotten <u>so that I can go home</u>. *is he trapped in the alley?*

And so with great disappointment, I slump over and wait some more.

And so she walks up to me.

She puts out her hand to help me up. I've met her before, but I can't remember where. When I grab her hand, she pulls me close as if asking to dance and whispers her name in my ear.

very interesting choice! really like this

Music blares from the violet box on the ground, reverberating off of the bricks on the walls that go on and on for forever. The music stirs us, so we dance for several <u>thousands of minutes</u>. Then the music stops, and she gives me a kiss. I kiss back, close my eyes, and place my hand on her cheek. It feels cold, and she smiles, her teeth bumping into mine.

I don't remember how long we kiss.

"How do I know you?" I ask.

She says nothing, hands me a key, and looks at the violet box with the keyhole on top. I unlock it. There's a blank sheet of paper inside, so I take out my pen and begin to write everything down. After I've written it all, I hold the paper up to my face and laugh. She laughs, too. Then she slams shut the box, grabs the paper and key, and runs.

I chase after her for so long that eventually, I can't remember why I'm running, and I try to remember, but I can't, and suddenly, I'm walking down an alleyway and see a box wrapped in violet cloth. *oh wow. trapped in same kind of never ending nightmare? this is a really cool story!*

SHEEP'S CLOTHING
Samuel Wampler

There's majesty about her when a bloke actually takes a look. Not glance or peek at her, but actually look at her. See her in all her glory, this motherly island. Her hills roll with grace and honor, they do. They swing back and forth, those mounds, and seem to rock the sky. Their green coats make them majestic, a magical green that pervades everything in the senses. It's everywhere, that clean vert. Clovers and grass, clovers and grass, flowers and thistles. Right now I'm watching two of her hills, searching the gap for any sign of what I'm looking for. Usually she has a flock roaming her pass, but so far, none this day. None this past fortnight either. She's been busy tending to other duties, and taking care of a flock demands some attention from her. Well, we can't be having that—she has her own children dying on her body. A man comes up through the two hills, and put him down, I did. His buddy looks askew at the body, and he went down soon after. The glen echoed a silence once more.

A clean method it was. No scream, no yelp, just a silent sleep down in the padding of her bosom. She'd take care of them from now on, I say. This island is in some bad sorts right now with her kids fighting each other, not much we can do about it though. They did something bad, and we pointed the finger, then they didn't fess up. Something about that makes a fellow's blood boil like sour beer. Da said our brothers would never get so far south as they have, but that old man's got the vision of a child. Not like he could sit at the table without a booster seat to prop his short stature. A couple more come up through the crevice, and they both go down just like their friends. I suppose they're friends. They're fighting for the same reason, no other but the fact they knew each other's family. Though I do envy them, those north-raping dogs. I'm all alone, and they get to die with friends. I'd rather be on the front, a rifle in hand, fighting with me boys. Fighting with Steven, fighting with Greg. I'm jailed here to this little hide, peeking out like a kid on a game of tag— 'cept I've got bullets for those I want to make *it*.

They were here to kill us. They were here, not because of their own thoughts, but rather the thoughts of their superiors. These boys didn't even know what they were getting into, like being told to patrol a cave while vipers nest in waiting silence. By being sent to me they were being sent to their deaths, and their superiors knew it. These boys were sons of this island, and being used like the sons of long-dead hookers. It made me cry many nights, but not a tear was shed. I held them back. Tears are for those who earn them. These boys are too young to even know what it means to be a man.

I didn't even grab a radio before I got dropped here. I could use with some music. Piano or flute, something that would make me feel an amazing bounty while patrolling her body. I've not been intimate even with my own wife as I am now with this land. I've got a blanket of her grass over me, keeping me warm. It's a bit nippy out at the moment, been so for nigh on seven count.

Had to kill and skin a sheep to keep warm, stick my hands in its entrails and scoot myself closer. The gut was radiating warmth through the night, and now that I remind myself about the sheep, could explain why the flock is gone. Old shepherd prob'ly thought a man was nicking his product. He wouldn't have been more right. The warmth of the entrails only lasted so long, and I had to scoot downwind and stoke an open flame. The sheep stomach was in my hand, fileted, and I stuffed some guts in it to make the sack plump. Pulled both flaps together and spun them a bit, then pinched them and knotted them fine. A fresh-killed sheep is good for warmth, but a dead sheep is only good for haggis. The skin was stuck to my body by dried blood, but I liked it. I had sheep's clothing on with grass on top. A hill in sheep's clothing. I'm naught but a part of her now—silent, waiting, and deadly. Her arms were wrapped around me, protecting me as she protects her beloved. This night before last was a queer one, but I still have that wool on me. No sane man passes up a free coat.

My first son will be born in a month or so. Been thinking about a name since being here among her cowl and tracks. Figured would name the boy Pride, I particularly like that name. "Pride Sylvatt is an interesting fellow," they'll say. I believe a name of the new tongue would be much better than Michael or

Cathal. Those men of the north have done nothing but make war, though for good reason. Those two names were owned by iron-mongering women-smothering bastards. All yields are at the cost of splashing the insides of our fellows on the surface of our gracious mother. This isn't no Christmas colors either, damned Catholics. That's the ticket; my boy will not be touched by the leprosied hand of a religious man, to save him from those ball-blasted lessons on kinship, legend, and castration. He'll be better off that way. He won't be thinking of God but of Nature. Nature is a lot more powerful, methinks. God will sit up in the sky and wag his finger—Nature will lob the fucking ocean or swing the earth at ya.

The day was winding down, but who am I kidding, I didn't know either day or night anymore. Just this scope. I had started a gait toward the kills so fresh from the yesterday, a troop of men not much older than boys. I could see a patch stitched on one of their uniforms, a token from his mum, most like. That doesn't stop me from rummaging in his pockets though. The boy had a pack of gum in his pocket, feces in his underwear, and a pack full of rations and ammunition. A sled would be helpful, I say, and fetched the one I had in me hide. The plank had gotten some work this past month, it had. Gathered three standard rifles and three sacks of food and bullets. I imagine when my time comes, people will find the pile of weapons I've been gathering. A gun for every dead man, it seems. Lest they come up from her bosom and grab their pieces, don't believe these rifles will be getting' any work on them for quite some while. Back in the hide, the sled was emptied in no short manner and then stashed away again until the hearse was needed once more.

I went back to the boys and stripped them to their nature. I burnt their unders in a flame and folded their other garments. The smell was of sweat and cotton, with a wave of pungent shit odor—and the tangy smell of burning nylon and plastic. A trio of jackets, pants, and hats. North emblems on them all, but that don't mean they don't deserve a funeral before being swallowed whole. A spade in hand, I dug deep and swift, three plots for three lost boys. A pop went off in me ear as I uncapped the safety on my knife, and pulled the sleek shiv out. The tip, so sweet and sharp, etched onto the bodies the numerals of sixty-one, sixty-two, sixty-three. A reminder of how many I've given back to her and a sign for those who discount us. Those who think they have lead over our lives. Those who dare to say we are not human enough for basic food. I gave them a savage's practice. I could scalp the dead, I could mangle their bodies—but I simply gave them a number. They were numbers to their army anyhaps. I threw their bodies into the earthen coffins and covered them over with her blanket of moss and grass and flowers.

No point in digging them in deep, a scout will be soon by here to check on their charge. I know because I can see the boy running this way through me scope. I'm back up at the hide now, waiting for revelation. Just listen to him bark out loud, without a voice and without a sound. It was the merry month of May when I left my home behind and left my wife nearly broken-hearted. I drank a pint of beer after saluting me father and kissing me mother to keep the tears smothered. Club in hand, I came here with my Frederic Special. The first sniper made by the blokes, they say. It be damned accurate. The scout went down short hereafter, saw his radio come up, so his body went down. No alerts, no more patrols. Set me free from this damn'nable place I've been stuck to. My mother here wants me back home with me wife and our coming kid. She don't want me slaying anymore of her livestock, she don't want me putting her lads and lasses to bed any longer. Though that's me imagining this land has life once more. I've stopped hearing her voice long ago, and now all I do is imagine the crickets chirp and birds sing. There's none of that no more. Just silence, that silence that makes you feel 'lone and afraid, that makes you want to hug a pillow close and sleep troubles away. None of that is happening.

A bee whizzed past my head as my eye hovered over the scope. Wasn't a bee though, seems the radio call got through more than I had wanted. There was a platoon not far behind that scout, from what is given by the sheer number of tiny thunders that beat upon his ground. Near on two-score of the livered felons wading through the Gates under my watchful eye. Haven't shot yet, deciding if living is worth it or not. I think of my wife and coming babe and the decision is sound. They be heading toward me home. Only one way to stop them. The rifle feels steady and calm, it holds my hand tight like a caring father. The rifle knows what was to come and it was ready, so I should be too. Not a second longer in that silence of marching steps did the doldrums of heaven resound. My mark fell but from him came a bladed breeze to shed her cowl from my body. These boys weren't trained in the art of marksmanship. Sloppy shots hit only the hill, but a bullet nicked the top of me ear to make me look like a gangy kit. I aim for necks, where the flesh is thin and bullet can pass through to hit another. Two went down together from a well-placed shot, then three, then six more. I was getting sloppy, and my shoulder had a bullet dug in deep and cozy. They were turning back now, dragging dead with them. Nearly twenty gone and into the earth once more. She has a humor, this island.

Feels bad.

There's a point a man can go to that teaches him mortality. I haven't quite yet gotten there, but I heard a fellow has to die. It's that brief moment when the eyes are wide with passion and fear, that moment when muscles twitch and shit and piss trail down the pant legs. It's when war is finally known to be a dirty sport, and that shit-covered pants would be the least of a fellow's worries.

My hands fiddled with the scope as I resumed my position seven-hundred meters away. The hills I've been watching, the Gates of Kurny some call them, are my zone. I've been here for two months, waiting, watching, and executing. I've been Godless since taking a man's life the sixth day by sending a bullet through his temple. They call me the wind. My breath has taken the souls of eighty-three. My shots are silent and my aim is true, so mark well my brothers—best you be staying away. I will kill you, I will send you back home to your Mum and Da in a natural box made from her body's majesty. I'll put you in that box meself and scribble a note so that when your brother-in-arms carry you, they read it loud and clear.

"The land will take you back, and it'll be greener evermore."

HEAT
Pamela Hnyla

"Set on fire, anything is beautiful," Frankie says. "And it all looks the same. Orange and yellow and blue flames." *? ??*

"And white," I offer. "Sometimes a little white."

Frankie stares past me, at his galvanized bucket.

I stretch on the sofa, rearranging my body against the scratch of the fabric, hoping the movement will catch his attention.

I am naked. *subtle*

He flicks his lighter repeatedly. His face glows more brightly than his Zippo.

I wait for him to reach over and touch my skin, but I've only managed to get him to fuck me twice, and he was drunk both times. Now even that doesn't work. *girl dump him ...*

Frankie pulls the bucket toward himself, throws in the packaging from his Pop Tarts and Skittles, his socks, my socks, my panties, a pile of used tissues, three cookies, and the newspaper I'd brought in from

25

the step. He lights an envelope and tosses it in. He bends over the bucket and, swathed in smoke, watches flames grow and heat and ashes rise. His eyes close, and his face radiates. *holy shit*

"What is it you want, Frank?" I ask once the fire dies. He had called *me*, after all.

"Gasoline, babe. Can you get me some gas? They're watching me." *on the run?*

I sit up slowly, pull my hair off my neck, and hold it in a pile on my head. I spread my knees, wide.

"What do I get?" I ask.

Frankie sighs and unbuckles his belt. I sigh too, and I push deep into the sofa and wait for the heat.

yikes. their relationship is rough...

these guys need help.

UNRAVELING
Michaela Tashjian

Jamie went to sleep brokenhearted and she woke up brokenhearted, but she did each of these things for different reasons. As Vern rose early to leave for the office, Jamie dreamt of the most precious of treasures—a baby—soft in her arms. Outside the apartment window she shared with her husband, the sky was dusty lavender. The child stirred on her chest; its head turned up to gaze at her, and there it was, the glistening look in its eyes that said, "Mother."

When the dawn drowned out the rest of the dusk, Vern's side of the bed was vacant, leaving Jamie as a modern day Hannah with no Elkanah to comfort her, no Peninah on which to cast the blame for her torment. So she rose from the bed, stepped into the overalls she'd cast onto the floor the previous night, and as she did every morning, met with an empty canvas in the kitchen.

Rubbing at the sunken prunes which were her eyes, she thought, *Vern doesn't love me.* She thought this as she pulled the damp kitchen curtains shut, and thought it again as she poured coffee out of the grimy coffee pot. *Vern doesn't love me,* she thought as she stared at the cracks in the wallpaper. It wasn't until her habitual pause before her first stroke of paint that she remembered what she had dreamed about: a real baby, hers. Helpless and loving. The motion of its outstretched hands came alive in her mind, tugging at the back of her thoughts.

—

On most days, Jamie's mind was with Vern, wondering where he was and what he was thinking about. She'd conditioned her mind to play his routine every morning. Just now he was letting himself into his office at work. He laid his suit jacket over his chair, hit the power button of the computer sitting across from him, and drummed his fingers on the desk as it started up. Here he would spend eight hours accounting for Trustco Bank, counting up their odds in order to make ends meet at home. He would stay faithful to her while here; if he arrived angry, he would use that to fuel his work momentum and take no notice of other women. Because when Vern told Jamie he loved her, he meant it. And he kept his promises every day. Vern always said what he meant, and meant what he said. If he didn't mean something, then he wouldn't say a word.

—

Jamie married Vern two years ago. They met at Wild Oak University, where Jamie had been studying art. Vern's major? Accounting. He would joke later on about what an odd match they were. Jamie would then laugh, but it made perfect sense to her; Jamie was attracted to broken things.

She noticed Vern first, in the library. He seemed so tortured, so different from what a normal adult should look like—his nose just a little too bony. Likewise, his glossy hair was not quite right, like a wig whose seams were sewn to fit a different shape of skull. In Vern, Jamie had seen gaps that could be plastered. Scratches she could polish.

—

This empty canvas awaited her every morning since they married. When Jamie was alone, she was in control of the person she was. Who was that person then, if not Vern's wife? More frightening than Vern's absence, though, was his *wholeness*, which wasn't there before. The way he woke up in the morning—so regular. He went to the office, came home, sat in silence, and called less when away. Those fissures he once had? She had plastered them with bits of herself, and now who was the broken one? Who was she today, without him?

She remained his wife as long as possible, making the bed the minute he left, smoothing the sheets and fluffing the pillows. Next, she cleaned the carpet and washed the dishes. When there was no more opportunity to be Vern's wife, she became his creator. First, she drew sketches of what he had looked like when they first met. She recreated the tiredness in his eyes, his weakened posture. After a few sketches of

Vern, Jamie did a study of him as a little boy, crying after his father hit him. This one was a little draining. Jamie looked back often on these stories Vern had told her, whenever she was angry at him for being so quiet. These stories had come up in passing when they were in school, during lunch before Jamie's next drawing class and Vern's Corporate Finance II. They'd been discussing a bill that just passed, a television episode, a celebrity found dead, and up would come a story Vern would tell her, of his father's physical abuse, the way his parents' tension would build until they couldn't take any more, and then spill into him—cornered. "Tell me more," she'd said.

Eventually, Jamie got around to painting him as he looked now, after being married to her for two years: his eyes larger, his hair a little coarser, less glossy, his skin the color of ancient parchment, cracked like mosaic.

She painted him as Orpheus leading Eurydice out of Hades, but Jamie couldn't come to put herself in the picture. She often painted a woman without a face, which is more accurate than any depiction of herself she could muster. For this piece, she painted the moment Orpheus looks back, the very instant Eurydice disappears. There was no silhouette or sign of her in the forest in which they walked, save a little glimmer of light behind Orpheus's back. *Did he collapse in the wood where his wife disappeared? Did he spend hours searching for her, in the leaves and behind the birches? Did he call her name or did he walk on?*

—

When Vern finally returned from work today, he found several new pieces in the kitchen. On the refrigerator hung a rough sketch of an infant, the word "MISSING" etched across the middle. Several paintings lay strewn about. Jamie had gotten the hair down perfectly: jet black, thick, and sticky. Jamie always got the hair down perfect. Her struggle over the eyes, however, lay evident in the accumulating copies collecting on the cabinet doors.

This continued for weeks. "He had your eyes," Jamie would whisper. He knew the voice she was using. She resorted to it whenever her throat was too swollen to emit real sound. "They were so shiny and clear."

The dream had changed her. Every morning the brushes and pencils would come out. Crayons, pastels. The descriptions at night, of the baby she'd dreamed about. *Their* baby.

A week after the first night like this, Jamie lifted her dainty hand to his face, her eyes searching his for understanding. But he looked at her the way one might look at an unstable gunman, or a drunk who stands swaying on a window ledge.

She even took pregnancy tests. Vern saw them in the bathroom wastebasket. Three of them, all negatives. One night he heard a sigh behind the bathroom door, and when he woke, there was a new stick stuck in the trashcan among the cotton swabs and acrylic-stained paper towels. He could sense the hope fighting within her, hoping the dream was simply a promise of something to come; he'd heard how pregnant women have dreams like that. But each solitary red line that came back threw up another window sash, calling—wake, wake.

He resolved to talk to her about it.

The next night when he returned from work, he found her in the bedroom. Having already slipped out of her painting overalls, she wore just her threadbare camisole. She greeted him with a warm kiss. Her hair was still tied up in a loose knot. Vern's eyes followed her slender white legs to the floor. Her toenails were painted red.

"Come to bed, sweetheart."

Once in bed, she leaned in close to him.

He said, "When was the last time you took your pill?"

—

Jamie was searching the history books. She re-evaluated her dream as a glimpse for the prize for which personal change would qualify her, and moved on to investigating honorary traits of motherhood. Sprawled across her studio lay *The Encyclopedia of World Mythology*, *The Brothers Grimm Fairy Tales*, and several versions of the Bible and world history. On her canvas, a pastiche of scrambled notes:

> *Medea: barbarously kills own children and flies off in a dragon-drawn chariot*
> *Eve: brings sin into the world and allows her son to be killed*
> *Hannah: begs God for a son and gives him to a priest*
> *Jezebel: Kills entire royal family, no.*
> *Lady Tremaine: No again.*

She searched the books for mothers like herself, but there were no orphan mothers to be found. There were many orphans, but nowhere was there any mention of these girls going on to have children.

Jamie had nothing more to scratch upon her canvas, and no more books she wished to open. She thought back to Vern, as she often did when reaching a boulder in any kind of activity. Back in her days in the orphanage, she had encouraged herself in the fact that one day she would adopt a set of parents by marrying someone with a mother and father. Thinking back on Vern's proposal, she realized it came as such a surprise because she hadn't met his parents, or visited his hometown, or learned much about his childhood, besides the painful stories about his father. She repeated this word in her head: childhood. Such an inappropriate word to use when speaking of Vern. It didn't match up. She looked at the calendar on the wall. Three days until he returned home. Jamie ripped the scratched up canvas from the tri-stand, and as she tucked the last history book back onto the shelf, she decided to find Vern's mother.

—

Green house—the quiet, carsick color of flavorless gum. The sidewalks outside matched the color of the cloudy sky, but were much more broken and worn. Scattered around were numberless bushes and weeds, but the evenly distributed streetlights gave the block a sense of order. Jamie had dressed up for the occasion, casting off her overalls for dark-wash jeans and an oxford shirt.

What kind of thing did someone say to a mother-in-law of three years when meeting her for the first time? Hello, my name is Jamie; I'm your daughter-in-law?

"Hello, my name is Jamie; I'm your daughter-in-law," Jamie said when the house's occupant answered her knock. All that stood between her and her husband's mother was a torn-up screen door. Jamie could see the woman's scalp through the tightly knotted hair. She was thin-faced, with the air of a woman who had not yet come to terms with time's indifferent passing.

"My daughter-in-law. Is that so?"

Jamie loved her already.

"Well, you might as well come in; I was just making some coffee." She held the screen door open long enough for Jamie to set her foot in the front hall and then let it go, leaving Jamie to follow her. "I figured someone would come around here sooner or later," the woman said on her way to the kitchen.

So Vern's mother was the type of person who talked to you from every room in the house. Not sure if she was expected to follow, Jamie waited in what appeared to be the living room. A piano occupied one wall; two arm chairs occupied another. Windows, curtains, a vase of flowers, everything a normal home had. Jamie turned around and saw a part of Vern she had never seen. He must have been thirteen in this picture, dressed in a red sweater and corduroys. In another picture, Vern was seated with a much younger version of the woman Jamie had just met, and a man whom Vern resembled. The man and woman were smiling. How odd it was, Jamie thought, that in daylight, monsters could appear so normal.

Eventually, the woman returned with coffee and Jamie managed to get her on the subject of her son.

"I did the best I could do with my son. Some people, though. He just wasn't as smart as kids come. His father and I loved him, though"—she spoke about him as if he was dead—"gave him all the pushing he needed to follow his dreams. All the money, too. Not enough, I suppose. You're the closest thing to contact we've gotten in five years, when it comes to our Vern." She didn't ask what he was doing now, or whether he was in good health.

Jamie sat forward and looked around the room when it was time to go. On her way out, a palm-sized picture frame caught her eye. She stepped a little closer to it and had to clamp her hand over her mouth, for there in the picture was the infant she'd dreamed about all these nights. The hair—so much darker than the ashy shade it was today. The eyes she had struggled for weeks now to portray on canvas—here they were in front of her.

She glanced around and caught a glimpse of the woman's varicose-veined legs walking back toward the kitchen.

"I trust you can find your way out of here, honey?" she called from around the corner.

Jamie snatched the picture frame off of the wall and stashed it away in her pocket. "Thank you," she called as she closed the broken screen behind her.

In thirty minutes, she arrived back at the apartment. She flung the mildewed kitchen curtains aside, releasing a torrent of light into the room, exposing so much of the dust that had stolen into her studio.

For three days, she awaited the return of her husband. She plastered the walls with clean canvas, mapped out his dreams on these, the story of their love on the ceiling. When energy was low, she painted rivers of red thread on every door. She traced the cracks on the walls with a startling blue. She spent hours replicating the eyes of that darling creature until she got them perfect.

The three days passed, and everything was calm when Vern returned to the studio. She kissed him where he stood. There was a hesitant taste on his breath, but his lips returned the gesture. He looked down at her toenails. The red paint was chipping away.

"How are you feeling? What did you do to our bedroom?"

"Hold on," she said. "There's something on your jacket."

She fastened her delicate fingers around the loose thread on his shoulder and tugged. It unraveled, stitch by stitch, plummeted onto the hardwood, coming undone.

COMFORTABLE
Jacob Harn

"Stop being mean to me," she says, dropping as far into the blue sofa as her long, light frame allows. She stamps a bare foot on the tiled floor and crosses her arms. Holding her elbows high, pushing her shoulders up, she exaggerates her passing mood.

Attentive to the words on the pages, he licks his finger before turning; he sits in the corner of the couch where the two sections meet. He closes the book, lays his head back, and watches the blades of the ceiling fan track the same line—around and around. On high, its blades indistinct as segments, the fan whirs as a whole: stirring, cooling, drying.

He closes his eyes. She scratches the blue fabric.

"Stop being mean to me." She says it playful and sweet, like a child asking her daddy for dessert before dinner. It's cute. It's disheartening. Her discomfort unsettles him as if it were his own. If she wants dessert, he needs it for her. *nuugh yikes*

he seems tired of her

"Baby," she says. He grits his teeth, careful not to show it across his face.

On her hands and knees, she closes the short gap between them. She lies against him, pulls and drapes his arm across her. Every bit of her loveliness presses into and warms the length of his side. She stares up at him with her sharp blue eyes, head tilted, frowning. He doesn't see this. The breeze pulses lightly against the back of his lids.

She wants something. yeah we know

Whatever the fuss is about, it's resolved. And it's done so without him.

The curves of her warm chest press just below his. The low hills of her ankles and knees give way to thighs sweeping into white shorts—bright against the darkness of her skin. He traces the map of cloth and skin with his fingers, needing nothing else.

She says something at a lower pitch. He knows what comes next, and looks at her, looking at him. ???

They kiss.

Their mouths move vigorously. Their lips press hard, without separation—indistinct as segments, stirring together. She slides her hand down his stomach, traces his zipper to the button, glides her lips to his neck, and exhales. With his hand firm on the nape of her neck, he tilts his head back again. The fan's blades still trail the same line. OOF

he just went back
to watching the fan.

BLACK CONVERSE, NO SHOELACES
Coe Douglas

We were waiting in the main conference room. I was staring at a glass of water on the big marble table that dominated the room. I knew that any quiver at the surface of the water was a warning that he was near. I learned this trick from *Jurassic Park*, and to us, his arrival was no less potentially terrifying than the arrival of a T-Rex. Only Silver didn't have big jaws, a big tail, and baby hands. He was freakishly short, had slicked-back red hair, and a mouth framed by a red goatee that was just faint enough to look like a rash.

—

Then the water in the glass rippled.

—

There was a moment of calm. Things slowed down for a second like in a movie—the calm before all hell breaks loose—and after I cleared my throat, everyone fixed their gaze on the glass. The surface of that clear, wet liquid quivered, then pulsed, and then everyone swung around and looked at the door. Silver was shouting before he even entered the room.

"There better be some fucking magic up on the walls or we'll be camped out until morning. And then, if there still isn't something that makes my dick go stiff, I'll fucking kill someone."

Silver barreled in, pushing past several junior creatives without so much as sensing their existence. He immediately went to the first ad. It was taped to the wall. That was how we did it. We'd work on a concept, then lay it out in an 11x17 ad to offer an example of the look, the feel, the tone, and the voice of the ad.

"Who did this?" he demanded.

"Merill did," I said. I was the Associate Creative director. I spoke for her. She was hiding behind a layer of Senior Art Directors who flanked Silver.

"I don't hate it. But it's not *there.*"

Steven Silver—whose unfortunate height and ownership of every season of *Mad Men* made my life almost unbearable—stepped to the next ad and immediately ripped it off the wall, crumpled it, and threw it at me. "Why even put that up there, Alan? Why? You want to fucking make my heart stop? Make a vein burst in my head? Don't even tell me who did it because I don't want to fire them right now!"

"Sorry, Steven. I—"

"Don't make excuses. Make my life easier. Filter! Fucking filter. That's why I pay you."

Silver looked at the next ad. He looked down and let out a painful exhale. He turned and looked around the room. "Whose is this?"

Silence.

He turned back to the ad. Studied it. We all looked down on the work, not metaphorically, but literally, because it had to be taped low on the wall so Silver didn't have to career his head up to see it. We'd always put it at *his* eye level which was unnaturally low for everyone else other than a child. Sometimes being around him made me feel like a giant.

"I asked who did this one." He didn't turn around this time. He just stared at the ad, his face now inches from it. Time slowed again. I think I started to sweat.

"I did," said Ray Brewer. "It's my concept. Mine and Scooter's."

"Well, I hate it more than the other one. I hate it so much I can't even bring myself to touch it. Can't bring myself to move. Yet the horror is so intense that I just can't look away. Still, I know that as I stand here, my soul dies a slow death, and what I really need most is that cleansing *Crying Game* type of shower to get the awful out of my hair. Who even fucking hired you?"

"You did," said Brewer.

"Huh. Did I? So even I fuck up now and again." Silver reflected on his words. The silence caused Brewer to laugh nervously. "Don't ever laugh in front of me," Silver said.

Brewer fell quiet, then melted into the crowd.

Silver hated the next ad, too. And the next one. I stood and walked near him now. He had a little bit of dandruff in his hair. I was looking down at it. It made me feel good to see it. Usually at moments like these, I would fantasize. I liked most the one where I grabbed the back of his red slippery head and slammed it into the wall, breaking his nose. Then, I'd spin him around and kick him into the granite conference room table. Others would join me, and we'd kick and pummel him until he was a bruised mass of flesh, a depository of all the rage and swallowed aggression I've had, we've all had, regarding Silver. I imagined that this would probably get me a blowjob from Merill. She's so beautiful. I imagined that I'd get promoted—because in fantasies there is no prison—and I'd be a far more benevolent ruler than Steven Silver. Plus, the work could be taped at a reasonable height, and our agency would thrive under my leadership. *Creativity Magazine* would do a story on me. My blog stats would blow up, and I'd triple my Twitter followers. It's a beautiful notion. I'm sure I'm not the only one thinking it.

"Alan, I gotta say this work is horrible! There is literally nothing here."

"Well, you kind of liked my ad," Merill said.

"Well, now I hate it. It's off-strategy and immature. The only thing right is the logo, and the client provided that, so don't be too proud of yourself."

Merill dropped her head. Damn, she was cute when she was having her heart ripped out of her chest. I got kind of turned on. Then, I felt brave.

—

Prison is nothing like they make it out to be in movies. There are a few less shivs, and far fewer risks with soap and showers, at least where I am. The guards are pretty friendly, and I'm totally high right now from the sedatives. That's what being an apparent suicide risk will get you. That and black

Converse without shoelaces. That part sucks. Of course, I'd never kill myself, but I am pretty psychologically broken.

—

In the conference room, I kept looking at Merill and how cute she was with her little quivering lip and pouty eyes, and I snapped. Things didn't unfold quite like the way I had fantasized. No one came to my aid. What actually happened was I face-planted Silver into the wall, but to my surprise, the fucking guy went nuts. Blood poured from his nose and he was dazed, but he turned around and punched me right in the eye, breaking my Ray Bans. I was pissed because they were cool and very expensive. Blind, I couldn't really fight like I had imagined. He punched my kidney, and in a fight-or-flight move, I ran like hell. He caught me, and I took a shot to the ribs. I was standing at the art desk now, so I grabbed an X-Acto knife. I gashed his arm, cutting his $150 Nordstrom shirt. That really made him mad.

"I'll fucking kill you, cut you up, and send your body to your family!" Silver screamed. "You seen *American Psycho*?"

"No, but I've read the book," I said. "Kind of overrated if you ask me, but I'm not a Brett Easton Ellis fan."

Silver screamed and charged me, and at that moment I realized that attacking Steven Silver was a bad idea. The rest was over quickly. Just inches from me, Merill was waiting. She hit Silver over the head with her old *iBook*. It barely worked anyway. The blow dropped Silver, shattering the laptop everywhere. The police were called. I got arrested. Silver went to the hospital. Merill was called a hero for putting an end to things before anything else broke. After all, there was a big pitch coming up that the agency badly needed to win, and there was work to be done.

—

I'm still in jail. Silver got out of the hospital after a few hours. Not long after the incident, he left the agency and started a boutique ad shop called *Silver*. A shrink named Dr. Claus said I suffered a psychotic break due to stress, over-work, and fear. I argued against the fear part and mentioned what a tyrant my boss was. My lawyer said, "Shut up and look crazy." So, I did. I got nine months in a facility which is pretty much a vacation for me. I have a stack of books, a big, high-backed chair, and pretty grounds with benches. My mom and dad visit every week. Merill, who got a new *iBook* and a promotion, sent me a copy of *The Savage Detectives* by a writer she's mad for named Roberto Bolaño. I think I'll read it now.

RECKONING
Meredith Raiford

There are three of me. More appropriately, there are two other of me.

starting off with mystery ... very cool

1

The first me that I am is in her second year at a state university nowhere near her hometown. She is not unknown, and enjoys being found, often advertising her arrivals. She is a nondescript (though pretty), white, adult, barely glancing into the trees beyond her family in their recent portrait. She spent her childhood and adolescence as liquid—a contortionist bending and flexing to the will and suggestion of her elders, egged on by the vain shouts of her peers. She subscribes to youth alone. When she smiles, as much gum as teeth shows; the ratio mars her otherwise attractive traits. She has never considered questioning her ears for truth. She will wear cowboy boots under her wedding dress, *you know, whenever that happens.*

very cool wording!

metaphor!

me, too!

45

*love this
wording*

She may have at one point <u>wondered whether a</u> <u>woman's lips were any softer than a man's,</u> but the fear that surrounded the consideration, and the better judgment that outweighed her first time drinking, assured she'd never know. (This is where her boyfriend managed to sneak an under-the-bra style grab and get his first *real* handful.) She drank warming beer from a day-old keg in an iced, industrial trashcan. (This was in a barely furnished apartment rented by his acquaintance from the baseball team; she spent most of the evening imagining where she might put a table, or lamp, and reconsidering the blood-swollen lips of the girl regularly taking gasping breaths away from her partners' face.) She wants to move her feet, or paint, for audiences. She may consider rushing Sigma in the spring.

2

The second me is the most unknown. She is a faceless, white adult, teetering between adolescence and adulthood, <u>nine-and-a-half years too late to feel</u> <u>comfortable with that much delay.</u> She spent three years playing a competitive sport virtually unheard of since the 1930s. She spent half of *that* time trying to figure out how to fully automate her grey cubicle, and the other half in an all black uniform dusting around oily men improperly using free-weights and women admiring the pulse of muscles in each stride. She may have also sold ladies' business dress clothes at that time. (This is where a customer admonished her for being too well-spoken to sell ladies' slacks and convinced her to enroll in classes again. This is also where she learned what a panic attack felt like and how to properly jiggle a candy dispenser to get three dollars' worth of jujubes for a quarter.)

The second me thinks the first me has a lot to learn. She prethinks every question she is asked. She smiles with her mouth closed, formerly ashamed of genetics and poverty that left her with symmetrical gaps between every two teeth, now left with an old habit of closed-mouth-smiling and mouth-covered-laughing. The romances she invents at stoplights never progress past the first kiss, as her intrigue has gone. She once ate nothing but navel oranges for a week.

3

The second me considers the third me the best me (but we've never met, and it's doubtful we will). The third me is *established*. She is distinguished, even in dreadlocks, with the same asymmetrical, small patch of grey that Maya Angelou started with. She is gatekeeper and storyteller. The stories and histories she holds are etched into her skin, and her hands move in the traditions of time. She is authored by the lines across her palms and the lines beside her mouth and eyes. She *is* an author. She wore a sensible heel and an elegant, efficient pant suit to her wedding at age 40. (This is where she decided she had everything she needed in her husband and her work.) She danced with abandon at her reception, surrounded by celebrants and colleagues. *love this line*

She smiles level, without gap or gum, and has no need to announce her own arrival.

I love the vocabulary and imagery !! So amazingly written!

47

NON-FICTION

SEAT 21B
Heather Peters

I seem to be the only one on the plane who's noticed that Martin Short is wearing Robert Redford's hair. They also don't notice that Ella Fitzgerald's dwarfish impersonator is asleep on my seat belt. The stewardesses have prepared us for take-off and are smiling at me, aware that I have not fastened myself in.

I gently nudge Ella several times, but the desired results only occur after yanking the seat belt from beneath her. The stewardesses carry on, smiling artificially at the next defiant passenger.

"Hey!" Ella shouts, pushing the hood of her jacket back and leaning all of her weight onto her left side. It's difficult not to laugh at her startled expression, so I wiggle the seat belt in front of my smirk as an excuse to alarm her, and turn to fasten myself in, taking a moment to size up the strange fellow beside me.

Despite the tell-tale hair, seamlessly sewed into his own scalp, Martin shows awkward animosity when a little girl passing by flashes her silver wings at him, beaming a snaggle-toothed smile.

"I got these because they're shiny and I like shiny, and I'm pretty 'cause the pilot told me so, and—"

"How nice," Martin says, glaring at the child's mother who is a living testimony for the events that the girl describes.

"He couldn't get over how pretty she is, could he, sweetie? And he's right, you're a perfect angel."

Martin shifts uncomfortably, turning red while they babble superficially. We both wait for a passenger to shout, "Amen!" and for a choir to burst into song.

I watch the interaction with delight until I feel my arm being pushed off of the armrest very slowly. I don't look over, just bend my elbow and orchestrate a spasm so that I jab Ella efficiently while I search through my iPod playlist, pleased once again with successfully keeping the old woman at bay. She passes out within a handful of minutes, nestled in the hood of her jacket.

Meanwhile, the little girl has grown bored of Martin, who is trying his best to ignore the adamant witnessing being directed toward him. I am the only one who is aware of his scalping skills. If they only knew whose hair he was wearing...

"I want to sit, Mommy," the little girl says, still looking at Martin, disappointed that he hasn't praised her.

"Let's find your seat, Princess."

"Yeah, go find your seat, Princess," Martin mutters down his sleeve.

I laugh out loud but look out the window when Martin looks up.

—

It's early in the morning, not long after dawn, and very chilly out. All of the passengers are bundled up. Despite the temperature and the fact that everyone is pretty cold, the air conditioning is streaming out above us, and there's a funny smell to it. It takes me a minute to realize, but I begin to suspect something when fidgety Martin beside me begins to finally settle down. I think they've put some kind of sedative in the oxygen as a calming solution for nervous passengers, which makes me anxious.

I tug the sleeves of my jacket down over my fingers and roll the material into my fists, holding it there until the stewardesses bring their trolley down the aisle, distributing beverages and treats.

"Coffee, please," Ella says faintly, nodding in and out while drinks are poured.

The stewardesses are carbon copies of each other with only their heights to differentiate them. They are pink-lipped Barbie-rejects from Stepford, and yes, they terrify me, but I ask for cranberry juice and a gingerbread cookie anyway and try not to make eye contact.

Ella comes to and notices that she hasn't gotten any sugar, so much to my annoyance, she flings an arm across me, trying vainly to get the stewardess' attention. She probably doesn't know that they're robots.

"I tol' her I wanted coffee, and she only gave me two creamers. No sugar," she pouts, deflating into her seat.

I hate Ella Fitzgerald and her coffee. I put my earphones in and turn away from her.

The cookies are dry and so over-spiced that my saliva turns them into masticated chunks of grainy acid, sticking to my esophagus. The cranberry juice is tart and cold, and it soothes my cookie-scarred throat.

Beside me, Martin squirms in his seat, trying desperately to make his limbs shorter in the cramped space, but he can't seem to figure out how to do it. I feel bad for him and want to tell him that his hair only looks kind of bad, not completely awful. But I don't because it won't make him any smaller.

Whatever it is they've put in the air conditioning makes Martin and Ella eventually nod off. Worried that I might be the only one able to fend off the stewardesses once they go rogue, I struggle to keep my eyes open and my elbow planted firmly between Ella and the armrest.

I turn off my iPod, but keep the earphones in just to dissuade the other passengers from trying to strike up a conversation. I should have brought a book.

Just then, Martin Short farts. It's undeniable. He has definitely farted, and it's only a matter of time before it reaches my nostrils and my face contorts or I gag, all depending on how foul the odor is. Maybe this is why he's been so fidgety. I panic, trying to lean away while also pretending that I haven't noticed anything. Earphones are still in, after all. It's not like I can crack a window or something.

I look around to see if anyone else has noticed, but mostly to make sure he's not trying to blame the act on me, like I would have done if I were him. But no one for several rows is awake, so I hold my breath and tuck my nose into my jacket, fighting back tears.

—

When I'm sure I can't take anymore elbow battles with the narcoleptic prune beside me, the captain attempts to make a landing announcement. I take out my earphones, trying to hear the bad news that is inevitably coming. Are we going to have to circle the landing strip for a few hours? Was the cranberry juice accidentally laced with a laxative? But the intercom is experiencing difficulties, the tallest of the stewardesses announces—over the intercom.

This is when I notice for the first time that Martin has been talking to himself for a good portion of the flight. I turn to him full-on, watching his face change as he switches from soft, sympathetic features to intense eyes and an angry red hue just short of bulging veins in his neck. He gestures fiercely as he responds to himself, only to be met with his own passive aggressive shrug and the defeated shaking of his head, disappointed with how his conversation played out. I glance at the ticket he's clutching to make sure we're not going to the same place.

We bounce in the turbulence, and as Ella attempts to sit up in protest of the ruckus, her hood slips down over her head, quieting her. She immediately nods off.

The captain's landing announcement comes through by some feat of magic that unnerves me when I remember he's been flying the plane. He stutters out an overzealous "Welcome to Atlanta, folks!" as we roll to a stop at the runway.

When we stand up to leave, I don't nudge Ella, although I really want to give her one last jab for old times' sake. I also don't look at Martin when he reaches up to get his carry-on, unsure if he's prepared a speech for me for not taking the blame when he farted.

We move slowly through the aisle, tired cattle looking to graze, and I wonder grimly what the connecting flight will be like.

HUNTING FOR WILD EMMAS
Carl Rosen

is he drunk?

Lighting is scarce in this bar, and I can't trust my eyes. I trace a coarse brick wall with my fingers to assure myself I'm on concrete land. People continuously bump into me. They try to walk between me and the wall, swerving as if on some vessel in turbulent seas.

A woman walks past me, making direct eye contact; she outstretches a surreptitious arm and cops a feel below my waist, then disappears into the darkness like she never existed. I immediately reach for the stable brick wall. *Who are these people?*

After traversing the outside portion of the establishment, I go inside to the most obscure section of the bar. I slide back a stool, and sit there for an uncomfortable amount of time without a drink, hoping to be noticed by the bartender—the only person I want to talk to.

As I sit there, I curse my friend under my breath. It's his fault I'm here in this purgatory while he's off

hire

"meeting up" with some girl. I can picture him sucking her face until her lipstick is smeared, as much on his lips as on hers. By now she has grinded his pelvic region to the point of genital retreat. I hope he contracts some embarrassing disease that mutates into a noticeable growth—I'd see it, I'd smile. I look around, envisioning the crowd disappearing with every glare I dish out. No such luck.

I'm elated to see a familiar face. I embrace my friend Allen, who thankfully can join me on this miserable eve. He attempts small talk about things that are irrelevant, but his voice functions as white noise—it's just nice to avoid my self-deprecating inner monologue. Allen begins to tell me about a girl he saw tonight and the white noise amplifies.

I don't know this girl he's blabbering on about. I don't know what color her hair is, what she's wearing, or what she smells like after working a nine-to-five. Right now she has the opportunity to be more than what reality can offer.

Her name should be Emma. She has oversized icy-blue eyes, which are magnified by unnecessarily large black-rimmed glasses. Her parents committed suicide on her fourteenth birthday in a cult ritual. Both of them. She's read every word written by Virginia Woolf. She thinks god is a figment of people's imagination. If she had to pick an idol to worship, it'd be the person who invented the tampon because they've had the biggest impact on her life. She only smiles six times a day on average. She's addicted to Cheez Whiz and semi-colons, and feels more guilty about the latter. She has the perfect amount of instability; it's a constant struggle between wanting to commit suicide and not. What depresses her most is her inability to imagine a creative enough way to go out. When she has sex, she's completely silent and blinks erratically—she requires absolute darkness and a loud fan. *thats so weird*

I've never wanted to meet anyone more, but she's dead as soon as I see the real her.

A couple of drinks later, Allen and I go to the outskirts of the dance floor, hoping to find her. As suspected, my other friend's tongue is so far down the girl's throat that I'm confident he can taste what she had for dinner. Emma is nowhere to be found, so Allen goes off searching on his own.

I imagine Emma brooding in a corner, with hopeful suitors barraging her with pickup attempts, and are all met with the same detachment. She's drinking whiskey because it gets to the point. It's a drink that says, "I'm not drinking to be cool or sociable; I need this because I'm broken," and with each passing sip she's able to stand up straighter.

I stand alone, keeping distance between the dancing and myself. A layer of sweat surrounds the floor, and I can smell the promise of sex. Its toxicity stings my nose and arouses me. Face after face is drenched in sweat and lust—it's a clothed orgy. I hone in on a girl with dark glasses and a tight, short, striped dress. I fetishize her in my mind as a sexy librarian and think about all of the books I want to read on her nude body. I imagine reading Nabokov so low on her lowly posterior—we would be locked in a room for days and she'd lay motionless as I read. I will have her. *THIS DUDE HAS ISSUES!!!*

I feel warmer and wobblier, and each step is less confident than the last. Control is now a lost commodity. This is me at my worst. I am here to kill. *?* *Hello*

The alcohol, percussive music, and rancorous smell of flesh transform me. I am a creature of lust, sent here to replace my fears and inadequacies with an object of temporality. I am a monster of repression sent to conquer, and this monstrosity isn't consensual. *Emma!*

I step onto the dance floor, maintaining an unbroken visual on my future victim. She is twenty yards ahead, surrounded by a small group of friends who are gingerly dancing. I lurk in the shadows, sidestepping obstructions in my path toward her. I anticipate her backward glances by blending in with the masses of people. She's oblivious to my presence, and song after song, I inch my way over. I watch her. I am so close.

She finally spots me and meets my gaze. She's already mine. I cut through the crowd and arrive beside her. *What will I do to her?*

I imagine her on my quilted operating table—my fingertips pattern her flesh as my hands sink into her skin. Fear and pleasure take over her face, her emotions televised on an eighty-three foot projection screen for my personal viewing. Beads of sweat urge her glasses to slide off, as she writhes on top of me. Each rocking second, the glasses inch further down her nose, until her hand surges up and keeps them attached. I imagine the aftermath: me lying in bed, eyes fixated to the ceiling in dissatisfaction. There is no happiness for me tonight. Only another distraction.

I'm already dancing with her.

I'm an awful dancer. I just stand there—the recipient of reverse-dry-humping. It looks like I enjoy the uncomfortable friction.

After enduring several minutes, I still haven't spoken more than three words to her. Every time I attempt to, she interprets my words of distress for whispers in her ear, and she increases her humping velocity.

The person behind me (I'm unsure and unable to check if they're male or female) decides to dance with us, and thinks it perfectly natural to be touching me. It's the conflict between moments of clarity versus instinctual cravings that inflicts the most damage to my psyche—the moments when the alcoholic haze dissipates, and I'm able to think, *this is absurd, my penis hurts. This place smells awful, I need to leave*, and then the contradictory, *sex, sex, sex.*

Here comes the perspiration. *Did I put on deodorant?* LMAO

We stop dancing. Her friends are leaving. I can feel sweat dripping into my socks. It's time for me to rip the clothing from her thin body. She asks to exchange numbers, kisses me, and leaves. The lower portion of my stomach begins to ache and my genitals feel more tender than they should.

My other friend left with the girl he was trying to eat, and I'm stranded downtown at 2:00 a.m. After calling a cab, I find a place to sit and sort out tonight's events. It's cold, I'm hungry, and viciously sober when epiphany strikes. Tonight's infatuation's parents are likely alive and she probably doesn't know who Virginia Woolf is. *Is it possible for me to be satisfied?* Emma is a mythical creature of sorts, and all I have is tonight's imposter, who now resides in my phone.

I send her an idiotic message.

goddd get help dude

TWEAK
Nicole Sundstrom

She didn't have to go inside to know what was happening. The constant rustling of her mother's sheets and the low creak of the bed frame told her that her sister, Nina, was violently shaking and writhing around to keep from thinking about the pain. She could hear the moans through Nina's gnashing teeth and knew she was probably sweating through another set of sheets, panting and crying.

very vivid pain imagery

"Help me!" Nina called out to their mother.

"They're on the way now, Nina," her mother said, exhausted.

You want help? This is your help, thought her younger sister. Agonizing or not, Nina made her choices, and it was time for detox. *yikes*

She never ceased to be amazed at her mother's strength and thought of how she would never have the patience to deal with someone like her sister. Her mother always argued that someday, when she had

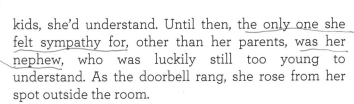

kids, she'd understand. Until then, the only one she felt sympathy for, other than her parents, was her nephew, who was luckily still too young to understand. As the doorbell rang, she rose from her spot outside the room.

"Come on, Davie, let's go play."

She shut the door behind him as the paramedics wheeled in the stretcher.

[handwritten: have her sister die? or is this her "killing" off her sister in her psyche?]

I had a sister once. She would brush my hair and dress me up. I was her favorite doll. She would use so much hairspray, pulling my wild curly hair hard against my scalp until it lay flat. I would clench my fists and grit my teeth to keep her from knowing when it hurt. She was my sister and I trusted her, so I never said a word. We would dance around her room to her Mariah Carey and Amy Grant tapes, stopping to sing in the mirror every now and then with our hairbrush microphones.

"One day I'm going to move to New York City and be an actress," she'd tell me, "I'm going to live right on Broadway, too."

"Me, too," I'd say confidently, eager to support her dreams. Eager to be like her.

Then I grew up.

[handwritten: switching between 1st and 3rd POV]

"Why don't you and my mom get along?" Davie blurted out.

He had attempted to bury it somewhere between talk of hamburgers and dirt bikes, but as a ten-year-old, he wasn't exactly smooth.

"It's hard to explain," she began, taken aback, "Maybe when you're older, you'll understand."

As was to be expected, it wasn't the answer Davie was looking for. She could tell he had been working himself up to ask her that question for a while, and she felt bad for disappointing him. Either way, she wouldn't even know how to begin explaining her relationship with his mother. How do you gently explain that mommy's a crazy drug addict? She grappled for whatever else she could tell him, almost forgetting the most important part.

"But you know that no matter what happens between your mom and me, it doesn't affect how I feel about you, right? You're my nephew and I love you."

He nodded and said, "I love you, too."

—

She did it time and time again: *I want to come home. It'll be different this time. I don't want to live under your rules. You'll never see me or my son again.* Your typical extortion. Unwilling to abandon Davie, an innocent victim of the situation, my parents usually went along with whatever it is she wanted at the time. She's not my sister. She's a liar. A drug-addict. A fading memory of someone I hardly knew to begin with. I have someone who isn't worth the time it would take to explain her role in my life. Or lack of one. I have to watch the silent pain eat away at my parents, literally making them sick. Unfortunately, for Davie there will come a day when it's no longer possible to overlook who she is. He'll understand the truth about his mother, but he may lose some of his childlike inclinations to forgive and forget in the process, just like I did.

—

She was finally in the double-digits, having turned ten just two months prior. She wasn't as close with her big sister anymore. Nina had her own friends and found her little sister to be a nuisance, as all big sisters typically do into their teen years. But no matter how hard she tried to be a good sister, to smile and be on her best behavior, she couldn't cheer her up.

She decided to give Nina her space to see if that would work, but it didn't. She was downstairs when she heard the loud slam of her door. Then the yelling came.

"Stay here," her mother said sternly, as she bounded up the stairs.

More yelling, but she couldn't make it out.

She got up and peered around the corner just in time to see her father breaking down Nina's bedroom door. Heedless, she joined her mother at the top of the stairs and watched her father wrestle Nina to the ground, slowly lowering the open bottle of nail polish remover away from her lips.

They sat for a while before her father felt it was safe to get up and leave. Unsure of where to go to or what to say, she decided to go after her father. She knew he would be able to make sense of it all, to explain what her sister was really trying to do—surely not actually kill herself. Wordlessly, she slid back the glass door, illuminating her father's crumpled figure

Head in his hands, shoulders shaking, he was crying. And no one made her father cry.

the stark contrast between these two paragraphs is sickening

Sometimes I think we'd be better off if she were dead. At least then we'd have closure. It would be hard for Davie initially, hard for my mother and father, but I've found myself wondering if it'd be easier than *thats* watching her waste away slowly. There's no such *bullshit* thing as a recovered drug addict, not from hard drugs anyway. Sure, they may stop using. They might make a fresh start for themselves. But that person— somebody's son or daughter, sister or brother, mother or father—that person will be gone and in their place will be a ghost. In their place will be a scarred, sunken-in version of the face you once knew, the face you once looked up to and even loved. But you'll know, every time you look into their dull departed eyes that they're just a cruel apparition of the person you used to know.

—

Muffled padding of feet skidded down the hallway at full speed.

"Nina," the little girl whispered into the dark room, "I'm scared..."

Bed sheets rustle in reply as Nina turned to face her sister. She was barely more than a mess of brown curls against the hallway light behind her.

"This is the last night," Nina sighed, as the little girl bolted under the covers next to her. *aw this is sweet...*

"Tell me a story about Morgan."

"I'll tell you one tomorrow. It's too late for that now."

"Please? I swear I'll go to sleep right after!" she begged.

Nina probably wished she'd never made up the story about Morgan, the little girl no taller than an inch, who had already been on at least one hundred various midnight adventures. Seeing as how she was already awake, Nina began the familiar story she had told for as long as her sister could remember.

—

We live in haunted homes, the families of drug addicts. Living with the ghost of the sister, the daughter, the mother you once knew, can make you susceptible to hope and that can be a dangerous thing—to hope in something that can never be. Others, like my mother, need the hope to hold on, even if it is in vain. For those out of hope, like myself, there's nothing left but a continual state of mourning. No closure. No peace. All we have are their ghosts.

—

"You'll be a big sister any day now," her mother smiled, running one hand over her daughter's thick black hair and the other over her taut abdomen. It was hard to believe Nina would be eight years old in a matter of months.

"I know. I can't wait to meet her!"

"How do you know it's going to be a 'her?'"

She wanted to keep the gender a surprise this time, but even with the neutral yellow nursery, all the blankets and toys were blue. They'd secretly hoped to have a boy.

"I just know. She'll be my little sister and I'll always be her big sister," Nina mused as she twirled around the living room,

"Well if she is a little girl, what should we name her?"

Nina stopped mid-pirouette. She wrapped her arms around her mother's belly and said, "How about Nicole?"

So, this was obviously a story about her own older sister. And yet, that doesn't clear up a whole lot? well, its "cleared up" but the lack of emotion or empathy towards her sister is disturbing

AMIDST THE BIRDS
Phillip Wentirine

Deep into that darkness peering, long I stood there, wondering, fearing, doubting, dreaming dreams no mortal ever dared to dream before.

—Edgar Allan Poe

I feel limited, confined, trapped. Monotony is suffocating me. I strive for change, to venture away from the repetitious memories weighing on me, to break out of the shackles restraining me, and escape into the unknown, the free, just in front of me...

But just out of reach—

Wake, eat, sleep. Repeat. I lie on my bed, buried beneath the dingy, olive sheets strewn over me. My thoughts travel deeper. I surface. *Exhale*. I stare blankly at the picture frames and décor on the white walls. *Inhale*. My lungs struggle to fill with oxygen. Light intrudes through the window.

Outside: grass, trees blowing in the wind, birds chirping, sun radiating though the clouds. A parking lot. The lush scenery is encompassed by the white bars inside the window, limiting my view. Next to the bed lie countless, opened bottles of liquor. I grab one; they all taste the same now. My buddy, Jack. The burn slides down my throat. I submerge back beneath the sheets.

My thoughts, my dreams, travel farther away from here. Crystal clear water, palm trees, warm, smooth sand, the salty ocean breeze, the blistering sunshine fostering relaxation, and the blur of reality. Here, I am free. Reality then invades my dream, permeates my limited bliss. I surface. Confinement shines back at me as I peer through the window. The trees no longer sway; I can't hear the birds; the sun radiates darkness.

—

I hear screaming outside my bedroom.

"Come here, bitch! You think you can just talk to me like that, after all I do? Don't give me that face, Cassandra."

"Stop, Chris."

"Don't tell me to stop, bitch."

"Get your hands out of my face."

It's a constant struggle whether to help mediate the tension or to stay put. Mom always tells me to stay put. I have the police station punched in on my phone. My thumb hovers over the send key. I clench my other fist with every shout.

"Do something about it, Cass. You dumb fuck."

"You're hurting me!"

The waiting with each passing scream annihilates my patience. I come around the corner to see my father shoving my mother into a wall. Her

72

figure slams perfectly into the previous indentions.

"Dad, stop! Why are you doing this?"

"It's okay, sweetie. Go back to your room," my mother's voice shakes out.

"What's he gonna do about it?" my father mocks.

I lunge at him. "Let go of her!"

He grabs my throat and pushes me to the ground. High-pitched shrieks violate my eardrum.

"That'll teach you to be respectful, you little bastard."

I reach for his face and kick his side with all my might. My father is twice my size. We continue to wrestle. My mother screams.

jesus...
— I cannot even imagine this
fear

That memory is still in my mind.

Never should divorce be a pleasant dream.

I reach for another drink. Bourbon. It does nothing to satisfy my thirst. *What time is it?* I continue to gaze out my window.

—

Julia *is* my world.

She found me when no one else did. My new life was empty. She helped me up when I found my knees shaking. She became my foundation.

Her pale skin, her dark hair, her awkward, quirky smile: she was perfect. Our late night phone conversations that lasted until I dozed off: perfect. Our cheesy, mini-golfing dates with salted pretzels and blueberry slushies: perfection hardly describes it. She made me appreciate the simple things in life. And that's where happiness stems from. Commonality.

The rush that struck me when I was around her. She was the source of the butterflies that never left my stomach. When I was with her, nothing else mattered. When we weren't together, she was my mind. I was obsessed, but so was she. Maybe that was our downfall.

Our intimacy was like fire, and we liked the burn. Our love for each other, if you can call our infatuation true love, was the ultimate force that glued us together. It was also what ripped us apart. She manipulated our emotions on the phone at night, twisted the reality of our relationship. She knew love for me was hard to come by, and she used that against me. Our bond held together by a cord that severed.

"Don't ever leave me, Julia."

"I can't imagine us not together, silly."

"I can't wait see you tomorrow."

"I'll see you in my dreams."

My nightmares.

That defined the depth of our connection. It's hard to hold on when you've never let go.

One day, I woke up, and she was gone. No texts, no calls. Nothing. I drove to her house, knocked on her door—no answer. Electricity surged though my body. What was false mixed with what was true; I knew this all happened too soon. Was I overanalyzing this?

My best friend, Nic, said to give it time, that it would all work out just fine; maybe she just needed some space. I just wanted her back.

Days went by. Weeks. Nothing else occupied my mind. It drove me wild. Did she ever love me? I went back to her house. I didn't knock. I went straight to her bedroom.

uh dude...

Julia *was* my world.

—

I stare back at my reflection glowing in the window. I look into my eyes. Sure, Nic. She just needed space... Partly my own fault, I suppose. I take another swig of vodka. I finish it off and move to the bottle of gin on the windowsill. It's night now. What day is it? Thursday? Friday? A week has gone by. I think it's a week. Time has no place here. I glance up to the stars and try to find the big dipper. The streetlights outside make it hard to see.

Nausea. It's been so long since I've eaten a decent meal. But I'm not hungry. I fall back on my bed and try to doze off.

I can't sleep. I toss and turn; exhaustion pumps through my veins. This repeats for what seems an eternity. I venture back into a dark abyss, a horrid daydream. But it's nighttime. A night terror. Another unfortunate experience graces my presence.

— *night terror are horrible*

I tried to get things right—for once. No matter what I did, how hard I tried, it didn't matter. Success was a foreign word.

I met this girl. Kara. "Fake it till you make it," she always told me. She took me to church. I believed in God, but I never considered myself religious. I went to a Christian school growing up. It felt like a prison. *amen* Nobody there was kind, genuine, like God would be. If this is what Christians are like, I don't want to be like them, I used to think. I thought maybe now I would meet better people; perhaps I would become religious.

I took on a second a job. It helped with the bills. I hoped one day to buy my mother her dream home. I didn't care for the people, but I tried to fake it till I made it. I was a hard worker; I always had been a hard worker. I made some friends. Good, decent friends were hard to come by. *good, lol*

Shortly after, my father got into a traffic accident and was rushed to the hospital. Despite the past, feelings change. People grow.

"Hey Jim, can I talk to you for a second? I have to make an emergency trip home."

"We have a company meeting tonight," he said without making eye contact, not stopping to share a moment of his time.

"What? I wasn't informed about—"

"It's mandatory."

"Jim, it's a family emergency. I can't just *not* go."

"Well, that's unfortunate for you," he said. "I guess you'll be out of a job then."

Some people, unfortunately, remain stagnant.

Unfortunate was becoming the cliché of my life.

Kara stopped taking me to church. I still believed in God, though. But clearly, my reasons not to were piling up. That was also a constant battle.

Decent people were really hard to come by.

—

I roll over in my tangled sheets. Crusty pieces tear at the skin below my eyes. I rub them to rid myself of the irritation. I suppose I fell asleep. The sun blazes through the window. Were these dreams or realities? The light glistens off the bottles surrounding me. But

I don't feel thirsty. I stare out the window, my usual to do list. I can't seem to see my reflection in the window anymore. It's like I'm not really there. I lose myself in the scenery. The birds in the trees, the parking lot.

—

The sound of the ocean breeze soothes me. The soft wind blows in my direction, tickling my forehead. The warm, grainy sand dissolves beneath my toes as I aimlessly explore the Earth.

"Daddy, Daddy, come play with me! I wanna go in the water, Daddy!" Ethan, my son, chants to me.

"Okay, buddy, let's get some sunscreen on you first. Don't wake up Mommy." My wife, Bekah, lies on a chair next to us in the sun.

Complete ecstasy.

Clouds begin to separate the sky.

What is it called, that feeling, that place you're at when your life filters into your dreams? That specific second when the two link together, that moment when they're almost interchangeable, where you lose track of the difference? Is this inception? There are bottles everywhere.

I drink. And drink and drink. And drink. It's almost therapeutic how distracting drinking is. What a beautiful nightmare.

Where did Ethan and Bekah go?

—

I wake up cold, sheets soaked from spilt alcohol, reeking. Empty bottles flood my bed. Was that a dream? It felt too real, too real. I drag myself over to my window. A reflection shines back this time.

Disappointment; selfishness; pity; regret. I look into my eyes. It shocks me.

I gather the empty bottles and pick myself up.

—

There's always a bright side to everything, just like the moon and the sun: eventually it will shed down some warmth, some wisdom. I say this sometimes, lying to myself. I know happy endings aren't always the case. But you've got to fake it till you make it. I used to have this idea that life was comprised of this complex formula, but as long as you could fill in the blanks, plug in the right calculations, at the end of the tunnel would be the answer. That karma really came back around.

I throw out the rest of the bottles and brew a cup of coffee, *good!*

I sit down, under the tree outside my window, amidst the birds chirping.

Of all the places in the word to fly, here they prance in the green grass.

Why here? I wonder. Then, I question myself the same.

PAIN AND ECSTASY
Krystal Davidowitz

It was 2 a.m., and I sat cross-legged on my bed with the phone in my lap. It was ringing again. It had been close to eight months since I last spoke to him, but here he was, attempting to make contact, just like any other day.

Honestly, I didn't want to pick it up, but I was tired of him calling. I wanted this to end, and the only way I could do it was by answering. I pressed the call button and held the phone up to my ear.

"Hello?" I asked.

"Mel?"

"Yup."

"Oh, God. Thank you so much for—"

"Say what you need to say, Ben." There was a long pause after I interrupted him.

"I'm sorry," he said in a low voice, and after a few moments, he continued, "I didn't think—"

"You're right. You didn't think. You took me for granted."

"No, I was just trying to make you see."

"See what?" I asked, my voice getting louder as my anger rose.

"To see how much I wanted you. Not just sexually... you, who you are, everything you were. I loved you, and I would've done anything to make you feel how you made me feel."

"So you thought in order to do that you'd drug me?" I yelled. "You promised that you would make sure nothing bad would happen to me. You were my best friend. You were my big brother!"

"I was taking advantage of you. I couldn't forgive myself for a few weeks. I just wanted you so badly."

"Oh, you felt bad for a few weeks? You're not sorry that you did this to me, you're just sorry that you got caught."

"No."

"How dare you try to call and feed me this bullshit?"

"Mel," he tried, "Please just listen to me."

I interrupted him again, "No, you listen. It's late and I have to work in the morning. I'm going to sleep."

"I'm sorry."

"I know."

—

"Are you ready for some Bassnectar?" Ben asked as he slipped the two Advil sized capsules into my hand.

I didn't know what to say. I was standing in front of the women's bathroom at the Hard Rock Café, and it was cold. I was beginning to regret wearing the cut off shirt and shorts combo. I looked up into Ben's eyes. He looked at me like a child, both reassuring and patronizing.

"How much is in each pill?" I asked. He laughed at me and threw his arm over my shoulders.

"Stop worrying so much, my little Keebler," he said. "In each capsule there is point two; just enough for you to feel it, but not enough for you to be stressing so much." He then gently pushed me toward the bathroom door while I put the two capsules into my pocket.

"Go."

I walked in and locked myself in a stall. I leaned against the door and pulled the pills back out. Inspecting them closely, I saw they both held the same amount of white powder, and it really didn't look like a lot.

I can do this.

I held both pills to my trembling lips and closed my eyes.

Stop being a puss. It's just a little Molly, what's the worst that can happen? Point-two is nothing. Just take a deep breath.

Ben's words resonated in by mind, "You'll have the time of your life! You said you wanted to do something you never thought you'd do in a million years, so here it is. Molly isn't just ecstasy, it's the purist form. Just a little will make you feel like you can fly. Plus, I'll be there to watch over you the entire time. I promise I'll protect you."

Taking one last breath, I popped both pills into my mouth and swallowed.

—

Two weeks later, I received a text message from Ben:

November 4, 2011, 2:51 p.m.
Ey Nick! U kno how I told her the caps
only had .2 in them? They really had .4. I
thought it would seal the deal but it only
worked for the night. What do I do?

What?   *HELLO!*

My hands began to shake but it never crossed my
mind to ignore his text: *what a freak!*

November 4, 2011, 2:52 p.m.
This isn't Nick.

Less than thirty seconds later my phone started
to ring. His name flashed on and off my screen, and
every time it disappeared, I saw the words, "I'll protect
you."
    Wanting his name and those words to disappear,
I ignored the call but cried out when he immediately
called back. Bile filled my throat, and I was lucky to
have made it to the toilet. I cried as I heaved, all while
that wretched ringtone continued to repeat itself over
and over again. After emptying all of the contents
from my stomach, I crawled my way back into my
room where the phone lay on the ground still ringing.
I sat up, leaned against my bed and stared down at it. I
picked up the phone and answered.
    "Fuck you." I turned off my phone.

what n asshole... poor Mel

Suddenly it was dark. Silence screamed as we all
halted, wondering what had happened.

No. It can't be over. Please come back. Encore. Encore. I need an encore.

The bass dropped, and my body exploded with goose bumps. The room began to vibrate from the intensity of the speakers. Running my hands through my hair, I smiled as the black of the darkness turned to sweet, scalding red. It filled my vision as I swayed my hips and dipped. I threw my head forward and slowly slid back up, raising my hands into the air. The red teased me and brushed its fingertips along my sides, across my stomach, and tickled my neck.

Come and get me, Molly.

"Ready for this?" Ben whispered in my ear from behind. I nodded and closed my eyes as he brushed my hair away and gently started to rub an ice cube he pulled from his drink onto the nape of my neck.

Oh my God.

My body burst with sensation as I shivered with delight. All the hairs on my arm stood up as the chill spread throughout my body. I sighed as I let my body relax to the touch. I was frozen.

Ben then turned me around, and through the red, I saw his gold, dilated eyes. He smiled and draped my arms around his neck. We began to sway.

Then I heard laughter. I looked behind me and saw a group of girls in the center of a dance circle. The guys around them were in a trance as the girls hypnotized them with their bodies. I looked back at Ben and took a step back into the circle.

I was a Goddess.

A reincarnated Artemis, I was on the hunt.

My hands started at my hips and moved up my sides, across my chest to my neck and in my hair as my hips told a story. I smiled to myself, feeling my energy radiate off my body and into the crowd. I

I'm glad she's so confident

closed my eyes to take in the moment, and when I opened them again, I was the only one left in the circle and around me, it had grown. All eyes were on me.

Yes.

Eyes belonging to both male and female were burning holes into my skin. I connected with all of them as their stares gave me more power.

Yes. I want you to want me. I want all of you to want me because I know you can't have me.

A phone popped up in front of me, and the red light that blinked said that others would be watching.

Go ahead. Save me. Immortalize me forever.

I dipped again, but this time as I rose, I felt his breath on my neck and his fingers grasping my hips. He pulled me closer and I leaned my head back onto his chest, eyes closed and sweat dripping. Ben and I had become one, and together, we held the audience entranced.

This was it. Nothing had ever felt better. As our bodies melted together the only thing that could tangibly run through my mind was pure and utter bliss. I turned around and pressed my forehead up against his. I smiled as he devoured me with his eyes.

The song finished, and the red disappeared. The house fluorescents turned on, and everyone began cheering as confetti and water showered us from above. I blinked out of my Olympian alter-ego and started to laugh. As I turned away, he pulled me back and kissed me.

This...

A flurry of confusion hit me as I accepted the kiss and kissed him back.

I don't...

When we separated, he smiled and placed his hand on my cheek.

"That was a mistake," I choked out. His hand dropped as I began to distance myself from him. Reaching his hand out for me again, he said, "Come home with me."

"We can't."

"We can. We can because I love you, and I would never do anything to hurt you."

I took his hand.

UUUGH !

what a shit stain.
I hate Ben !

OATH BREAKER
Raptor Grant

One word to define Jack Leach: Impossible. Impossible because one word alone could not describe the contempt that stewed in my bowels. And when his father was reassigned to a different Naval base, I cried. Jack Leach was one year my junior and had just finished fifth grade; I wanted to be around when he entered Brewster Middle School so I could relish in the torment he'd receive from his peers. Dreaming about his humiliation was the only thing that kept me from smacking that foolish smile off his face. At the time, there was no one I detested more.

On my honor

There he was. Again. Jack Leach could never take a fucking hint. Doddering along with farm boy blonde hair and a smattering of freckles that some inebriated deity slapped on his face. And ruby lips, crooked in a jackass's grin.

"Hey, dude."

"What?" I averted my eyes to avoid melting my mind.

"I'm leaving."

"Then what are you still doing here?" *why is he mean to him?*

"I mean my family's leaving."

An apology poked its ugly head out of my mouth, but I busted its face with a shovel and it scampered off.

"'Bye then." I walked away, leaving him standing on the sidewalk in front of our houses on Wavell St.

"'Bye."

I heard a clatter against the pavement. Two halves of a carved walking stick rolled toward me. I dismissed them.

I never saw him again.

I will do my best to do my duty

I propped up the tent as my fellow Scouts did the same. They laid claim to their patch of dirt, marking their territory with primordial devices like camping chairs and tarps. We were barbarians.

We camped once a month, as was custom with Troop 597, and this month our chosen terrain was on Camp Lejeune, the Marine Corps base where we held our weekly meetings. The campout was more of the usual: field activities like pioneering and orientation during the day, telling ghost stories and breathing in *gross!* noxious smoke at night. For breakfast, we cooked omelets in Ziploc bags, and for dinner, we roasted potatoes in aluminum foil next to fading coals. All was in order.

Until Jack Leach.

It was the second night. We were given orders by the senior patrol leader to start breaking camp so we could be ready to depart in the morning. Some of my fellow Kodiak patrol members had tried their damndest to build a tree fort earlier that day. Along came Jack Leach, in regulation shorts that showed a tad too much pale leg for my comfort, tearing down the construction, limb by limb.

To be honest, I didn't give a damn about the fort. Jack Leach's enthusiasm just pissed me off. Happy and carefree, as if he'd forgotten the irrevocable injury he caused.   *???*

"Knock it off." I shoved him, and he fell on his ass, snapping his favorite walking stick.   *you broke his stick!!*

Jack Leach pounced in my direction, coming at me like Boris Karloff, nubile arms outstretched and silent murder dancing in his eyes. Or was that just the reflection of the campfire?

Either way, he was a bull at Pentecost, and I was the simpering churchgoer who wasn't smart enough to not wear red.   *such interesting word choice*

Luckily, the other Scouts caught wind of Jack Leach on the warpath. They were on the lookout for it, since I'd had several altercations with him before. The senior patrol leader, Wade Marsh, stood between us, talked Jack Leach down, and admonished me for agitating him. He deserved it, didn't he?

To God and my Country

My first campout as a Boy Scout. I graduated from the Webelos and should have been excited. Eleven years old and feeling proud. But my tentmate, Douchebag, decided to switch accommodations with another member of our patrol and guess who took his place in the cramped pup tent. Jack Leach. I didn't hate him; I'd just been avoiding him. I didn't want to discuss what happened last month, or the thoughts frolicking in my mind.

We camped in an acre of farmland that belonged to Wade's uncle. I was setting up the tent, crushing the stakes into the ground with my foot, struggling not to notice the stiffness of the stake or its tapered length. Enter Jack Leach with a walking stick. Words were carved along the shaft, a bygone pledge. Jack Leach waved the rod back and forth, probably fighting off imaginary foes with a make-believe sword. He lost control and whacked me in the back of the head, on the very spot where I had recently acquired a scar. *oof* "Goddammit."

I chased him around the camp, my eyes planted on his backside as I endeavored to throttle him. Some of the other Scouts managed to calm me down before I did any damage.

The next morning, after the breakfast fires had been lit, Jack Leach was fiddling with a propane tree and accidentally loosened a valve on the tank. Propane hissed over the fires. We all fled to a nearby creek, praying with stupidity that submerging ourselves would protect us from the impending explosion. It never came. As we ran in one direction, Wade ran in the other, toward the propane tank before quickly tightening the valve. I couldn't believe Jack Leach could be so fucking stupid. *this narrator is unforgiving*

To obey the Scout Law

I was new. My father, a doctor in the Navy, was reassigned to Camp Lejeune; we moved from Houston to a small city adjacent to the base. My parents wanted me to continue in the Cub Scouts, so they enrolled me in one of the base's Packs. Pack 597. I walked into a Methodist Sunday School room, picking out my peers, outfitted in the exact same uniform as me: green socks with red trim, forest colored shorts, a tan buttoned shirt, and a yellow kerchief.

The other kids were already engaged, conversing about how they spent their summers. The Pack Leader introduced me, and I found a seat, apart from the rest.

As Webelos, we were at the final verge between Cub Scouts and Boy Scouts. The last two years. As such, we had to memorize different elements of the Boy Scout creed: the law, the motto, the slogan, and the oath. *had to do this in JROTC ...*

The Leader glanced in my direction and said, "Last week, we went over the twelve points of the Law. I know you're new, but do you know any of it?"

Silence.

"It's in the handbook."

I tugged at my neckerchief. I dreaded looking like a fool.

One of my peers sat down next to me and muttered under his breath, "Trustworthy."

I repeated the word to the Leader, followed by the other eleven points the kid fed me. Trustworthy, Loyal, Helpful, Friendly, Courteous, Kind, Obedient, Cheerful, Thrifty, Brave, Clean, and Reverent.

I turned to give my thanks.

That's how I met Jack. *So then, why are you so cruel*

To help other people at all times *to him?*

A year had passed since I joined Pack 597. My family was moving again, but this time only twenty miles. We were moving onto Camp Lejeune.

We turned on Wavell Street, and there was Jack. Playing in his front yard. Only two houses down from mine.

Our eyes met. We both smiled.

Over six months, Jack and I became close. Not best friends, but that didn't stop Jack from trying.

"Are we best friends?" he would ask on a weekly basis.

"We're friends. Isn't that enough?"

"I suppose." He glanced at the sidewalk as we walked from the bus stop to our homes. Suddenly, he ran into a nearby yard, grabbing a branch. "Just the length for a walking stick." *he always seem to have*

I was envious. It was a nice sized branch, and *are* once whittled down, it would make a cool staff.

"Are we still on for the sleep over?"

"Of course."

We had a sleep over every other weekend. We alternated where we slept since we both had twin beds in our rooms. But every time Jack spent the night at my house, he would break down into a torrent of sobs and tears. This was a tradition of his, not only at slumber parties, but also on campouts. Whenever he was away from his parents, he always thought the worst. *:(he's just a baby*

"Hey, are you awake?" he asked one night, as we were bunking down.

I snuggled deeper into my sleeping bag, trying not to think of all the tiny critters that could crawl into the foot space. "What's up?"

"I'm scared," his voice wavered.

"Again?" I asked.

wow. he needs therapy

"What if my mom and dad die while I'm gone?"

"I'm sure that's not going to happen. Go to sleep."

"But it could. Mom's already sick. And what if Dad gets into a car accident? Or dies in a fire?"

I turned on a flashlight, shining it toward Jack's fetal form.

"Listen. They're not going to die. Not tonight. And even if they do, what can you do about it?" *dude.*

Apparently, that was the wrong thing to say because Jack broke into even louder sobs. I didn't want any of my other friends to hear this. I wanted to spare Jack's dignity as well as my own. I reached out an arm and touched Jack's shoulder.

"It's going to be all right. I'll keep you company until you see them again."

"Don't leave me alone."

"Don't worry. I won't abandon you. We're friends."

"Promise?" *oh no...*

"Promise." *This is tender..*

He grabbed the staff that he always kept close at hand. He had stripped the bark, leaving an ivory surface. "Promise on the stick."

I sighed. I wanted to sleep. "I promise on the stick."

To keep myself physically strong

It wasn't just sleepovers. Every day after school, we would ditch our backpacks stuffed with assignments and head up to Jack's room to play with Legos, tackle Aladdin on the SNES, or duel with Pokémon cards. Honestly, I think Jack only got involved with Pokémon because I followed it. He cultured his

hell yeah, pokemon!

hobbies off of those around him, never finding his own footing, his own niche. He just wanted to fit in.

Soon, we started exploring. We'd hike into the woods, run through the backstreets of our neighborhood playing Cops and Robbers, or go biking to the dollar theater. And then there was Gross Club.

Between our homes, a two story house was being renovated by Lejeune maintenance, so the walls were stripped away, leaving a skeleton of support beams and timber. Jack led the expedition, daring to enter the house, and for once, I was the one who followed. On the second story, we set up shop, forming a club between the two of us. We would dare each other to do the weirdest things we could think of: urinating against pieces of wood, stripping in front of each other, and kissing local girls on the cheek. Thus, Gross Club was formed. Jack spent time carving the words "Never Alone" into his stick. We began every Gross Club meeting by swearing friendship and loyalty to each other, our hands placed on either end of the totem. And our bond had never been stronger.

Mentally awake

"Have you ever done it?"

I looked up from my Legos. "What?"

"Have you ever, you know, had sex?" Jack whispered the last word with taboo glee.

I shook my head and buried my focus into the building blocks. I was constructing a Fortress of Solitude.

"Do you want to?" Jack's eyes were fixated on me with a manic stare.

94

"No." I said it simply and honestly. I thought that would have been enough.

"Please," he pleaded.

I repeated my answer.

"But we could just go in the closet, take off our clothes. It would only be five minutes." *uhh dude*

I glanced toward Jack's door and eyed the lock. I calculated the probability of Jack's father walking in on us. Then, I realized that I was actually considering Jack's request. I just couldn't do it.

"Sorry."

"I won't be your friend anymore." *dude! manipulation*

And that hurt. It hurt because we had built up a bond, a strong friendship, and he was willing to throw it away because I wouldn't have sex with him. I was only eleven years old. And so I decided.

If he didn't want to be friends, so be it.

"Fine." I started to leave.

Jack sprang up. "No, please, I was just kidding."

I relented. I stayed. And the topic never came up again.

What if? That question plagued my mind every night, casting twin fogs of doubt and wanton abandon. One thing was certain. He wasn't my friend Jack anymore. He was a foreign entity decked in a grotesque smile. An alien thing named Jack Leach.

ok... like I get it was shitty that he manipulated And morally straight *you but like ...*
harsh

Jack had moved away. But thoughts of that day have lingered in my mind ever since. I wanted to say yes. *did you?* After a soul search lasting seven years, I knew I was gay. I never should have destroyed the link we forged. He had asked a simple question. I had tormented him for the rest of the time I knew him. I tried to find the broken pieces of the walking stick, but ended up only finding one half. I keep it as a reminder; the word "Alone" carved into my memory.

One word to define the relationship between Jack Leach and myself: Impossible. Impossible because one word alone could not do justice to the shame that suffocates my lungs.

really good line

HOPEFULLYS
Alexa Oliveras

Nothing gold can stay.

—Robert Frost

At seventeen, Carly lived weekend to weekend. She raced through each day in search of something. Strings of twinkling lights. The stretches between shimmers. The waiting places.

We struggled with our own words, while savoring the last remnants of hers on our tongues. Her voice hovered above others.

The day-to-day minutia of school and senior year receded far beneath her notice. Our struggles to get into college made her eyes roll. Marie and I struggled through midterms while she dreamed of music and tattoos. I'm not sure we had the better perspective.

When Carly came to school for the first time in weeks, eye bulging in its socket, we figured she was sick.

oh no ...

"The doctor says there is a mass from a sinus infection pressing on my eye. Apparently, I'm missing a bone plate behind it." Carly talked like it all was some ironic joke, one big inconvenience.

"So, what are they going to do about it?" I asked.

"I'm going in for surgery in a week. The only way to remove it is to cut into my head. I just want to go out on my parents' boat Saturday and then go see Copeland play at the Pearl. Not be in a hospital bed." I didn't know what to say.

I looked at her eye again, it really didn't bulge that far—maybe three millimeters. Even so, it threw off the proportions of her face.

"The school threatened that I won't graduate if I miss any more classes. Just watch, I'll have fucking cancer behind my eye or something," she said a few days before surgery. We laughed, because she wanted us to. She wanted us all to marvel at the level of shit her life had descended into. We let her make grand assumptions and applauded her for her callousness.

The doctors found it during the surgery, with her skull open on the table. The mass, the supposed sinus infection. She woke to find the stunned face of her father, her mother's hand gripping hers through the sheet. The biopsy showed a soft tissue cancer common in children.

Carly never came back to school, not as an enrolled student.

Visiting us in class, after a series of intense chemotherapy treatments, she wore a knit hat over the white dome of her head, and sat in a desk at the front of the classroom, eyes and face puffy from the medication. A C-shaped incision hid under her hat. She spoke more slowly, with less cynicism. She looked around the room as though she was only just returning after many years. She wouldn't be returning for senior year; graduation and college hovered in the way off distance, in a land of hopefullys.

She spoke to us with the same bruised wisdom our teachers and parents used. "I spent so much energy hating it here, hating every minute of it. And now the only thing I want is to be here with you guys," she said. Her mom sat nearby, never more than a few feet away.

—

Graduation came and went. One girl, who we never knew was pregnant, gave birth in June. She had hidden the growing bump under a baggy sweater we never questioned, even during the warmer months. Marie tattooed an hourglass on her foot with the chain wrapping around her ankle. We ate sushi. Some started smoking. Or picked up knitting. We bought ukuleles or harmonicas that were proudly displayed but soon gathered dust in corners. Suddenly, we became freshman again. Our lives plodded onward. Carly stood frozen in ice, battling the cancer that once was just an infection.

—

Marie sits across from me, complaining about the waitress—how in France they leave you alone. "Can't she see we're talking?" She has put the nose ring back in, and a tiny tragus piercing dangles from her ear. Her hair is no longer the fire orange it used to be, instead a more muted burgundy. We spend a long time talking about our new majors, comparing professors, loans, and summer trips. We only meet a few times a year now, barely keeping touch in between. She is one of a few from high school I keep track of.

Inevitably, we end up on the topic of Carly.

"There is this girl in my Art History class. She told me her boyfriend has brain cancer. She quit her job and uses the time to take her boyfriend for treatments and scans. I can't imagine dealing with that right now. I started telling her about Carly, but then I remembered..." I trail off.

"Yeah, the last anniversary of her death was really hard," Marie says.

I nod quietly, picking at my omelet.

"I have cervical cancer," She says between sips of her latte. A minute goes by.

I stir my coffee.

"Is that why you're in town, for treatment?"

She cuts her pancakes into small pieces.

"I found out I had HPV about a year ago. After a couple abnormal paps came back, they biopsied for cancer." She tells me all about HPV, about how her roommate caught it too but was fine. Marie's body didn't fight off the virus. She tells me she is a genetic dead end. She won't be able to have children. She says all guys eventually want to pass on their genetics, the family name.

"My mom has a friend with cervical cancer, they caught it early," I tell her. "She had a baby last year. So you never know."

"Those are the stories I like to hear."

She's sick, but not sick like Carly. Neither of us thinks she's going to die. She's being treated. I tell her to let me know how her next checkup goes.

"Are you still with that Alex guy?"

"He said that it was too much stress dealing with me being sick. And it wasn't like we were married, so he didn't have to stay and take care of me. He broke up with me right before my first treatment."

"What an asshole."

"I know. I'm in the exam room and the doctor is elbow-deep in my vagina, my legs are in stirrups, my boyfriend just dumped me, I'm completely alone. So I start sobbing, hysterically. I can't imagine what the doctor thought. She just looked over the sheet and asked me if I was going to be okay. She must have thought I was in pain or something. She probably just thought I was crazy. I tell her I'm fine, just go back to lasering the cancer off my cervix."

"You should have told me. I would have come."

"I know. It's fine. I got through it."

In the parking lot, Marie and I say our goodbyes. We hug a little more tightly than before. She won't be back until winter break. We linger near her car a while longer than we normally would. Finally, she gets into her car and drives away. For a moment, I'm in that classroom where we all sat savoring each breath, our healthiness—frozen in the terror of any alternative. Then, I'm back in the parking lot, the slow drizzle settling on my cheeks and shoulders. I hurry to my car, late for class.

AND THE OTHER, GOLD
Caroline Fraley

It occurs to me now, rushing to the bridge, that he might not be there. I am only ten minutes late, but Joseph isn't the type to wait around.

"Sunshine," I hear from behind me. I whirl and see a skinny figure leaning against the step railing. Cigarette smoke twists up around his soft and dirty curls. He looks the same, maybe a bit rougher than I remembered him, his hair shorter, his face thinner; but the skull bandana and one earring dangling girlishly to his shoulder haven't changed. Somehow at 23 he still reminds me of a high school boy from the '80s—giving the impression that he's all in leather even in slacks and a t-shirt.

"Mr. Joseph Gaston."

"Miss Caroline Fraley." He grabs me around the waist and pulls me into him for a long hug before pushing away to examine me. "You look good," he says finally. "What happened to your dreads?"

"Cut 'em off about a month ago. You like it?"

"Looks good. It was short when I met you, remember?"

I remember very well. We'd been students together at North Greenville, a strict Christian school—one that painted thick red lines around each of the dorm buildings that the opposite sex couldn't cross; one that would fine you if caught smoking cigarettes, even off campus.

Four of us smokers found each other and established a meeting spot at an abandoned building project. Me, Joseph, Todd, Haley. In love and inseparable. When campus police caught us there, we downsized to a trailer we found in the woods. Spliffs, flasks of whiskey, and prescription pills found their way into our meetings. We started to party harder. Our group grew; things got wild. Eventually, we all dropped out and moved into a house downtown with Todd's deadbeat father.

It's funny to think about it now. We were classically young and reckless; we thought we were something special. It would be much later before I realized how many low-lifes do the same old things. Haley was the first to go, then Todd. I held out till the end of the semester, but eventually I went, too. Joseph was the last to give in. And when he finally did drop out, we didn't hear from him for months.

"Do you want a smoke?" I hear him say now.

"Benson and Hedges?"

He nods in a southern gentleman kind of way—*yes'm*, I hear in my head. To this day, I don't know anyone else under fifty who smokes Bensons. "Of course you do, country boy. Nah, I've got my own."

We walk across the street to *Chicora Alley*. It's my favorite bar in Greenville, perhaps in South Carolina. I kiss the bartender on the cheek, and he says the first round's on him. Beers in hand, we make our way to the end of the bar next to the Miller High Life sign, the same sign that got stolen last year during peak bar hours and then mailed back from a Louisiana address a month later. Things, like people, tend to come back around.

Joseph wants to know if I've talked to Todd.

I have. He's in rehab in Utah for heroin. Clean six months now and doing well.

Haley?

A junior in elementary education in California. Finally came out as a lesbian.

That little rascal.

I know.

And you?

Doing well. Managing a restaurant in Jacksonville these days. Just found out I got back into school; start in August. How have these years treated him, I want to know.

He doesn't answer right away but looks around for something to fiddle with, eventually asks the bartender for another round.

"Oh, so you've got money now?" I wink at him.

He glances up to see if I noticed his smile and struggles to smother it. "I'm a working man these days."

"Oh, really?"

"Well, not a real job. Just my parents' farm." The way he lowers his voice and mumbles the words makes it seem like a confession. I'm reminded I've never seen the farm where he grew up. Once, I drove him an hour to Dakusville when he found out his Dad had lung cancer. He had me drop him off on the outskirts of town where he could walk the rest of the way. What were his parents like, I asked him. *Country.*

"You were all out-and-about last I heard. Why the move back home?"

"After you moved away, lady, I got locked up for a while." He seems to hesitate. I imagine he's debating how much to tell me. "I got caught shoplifting at Wal-Mart—beanie weenies and shit 'cause I was hungry—and when they got me they found my ice. They made me cut off my hair, those fucking pigs." He laughs.

It's no big news that he's into meth. We'd found out later that's where he'd been those months we didn't hear from him. But even still, the thought of him pale and sweating in a house full of low-lifes, smoking ice, losing weight, losing his teeth, wanting so much to sleep and not being able to—it made my stomach tighten. I try to think of something lighthearted, but nothing's coming. Instead, I order another round. "And give us some Jameson shots while you're at it. Three, if you're in."

Laughter and small talk take over. Friends filter in and filter out; some take shots with us. We go out back for a smoke. Outside, the street lights stare indifferently, save one, sitting at the corner rasping insults through the alley. I roll a cigarette quietly.

"I overdosed on heroin last month," he says, lighting his smoke.

"You what?"

He laughs, and I catch his eyes. Despite his struggle to sound nonchalant, there's something arresting in his gaze, something in his eyes that I can't place—the word *pleading* keeps coming to mind.

"How did it happen?"

I watch as he runs his fingers around the glass as if feeling for a label to peel. This boy who's so tough, who doesn't let anyone close to him, just seems so childlike for a moment I have to fight the urge to wrap him up in my arms.

"It wasn't difficult, if that's what you mean." He flips his hair out of his eyes. "After I got out of prison, my tolerance was down. I was in my room, bored, and decided to shoot up a gram and a half of raun. My sister—fucking bitch—found me later."

What does he want me to say to this? I think that someone else, someone better, might know the right thing to do. People get their bachelor's degree in this, study the right ways to respond in this kind of situation. As for me, I've known friends to overdose. But in those times it was different—different because I didn't have to answer to them like this afterwards, and different because they had been people from whom I'd expected it, I suppose.

No. That isn't it.

Suddenly it occurs to me that it feels different because *he* feels different.

An image flashes of the two of us locked in his dorm room bathroom at 4 a.m. His roommate is gone, and Haley and Todd are passed out. We'd started the night in the car, but there was snow on the ground and we couldn't take it, so Joseph went in and opened a window for the three of us to climb, 24-pack in hand, into his room.

The way he's sitting with his back twisted around the bathtub spigot can't be comfortable. We have to wrap our legs around one another to fit into the empty tub. It's awkward with a skirt, but somehow I don't mind.

"So," he starts, tapping his cigarette into the glass jar. He shivers. "Jeez, it's cold. Are you as cold as I am?"

I reach my foot to kick the spigot.

"What the hell!" Joseph yelps at the icy stream and curses again.

I laugh at him, hard until the water quickly turns warm, then hot, and fills the tub. We lay back and listen to the music.

"How was your sister's wedding?" I ask finally.

He shrugs. "Didn't go."

"Joseph! She's your sister!"

"So? She's a bitch."

I open my mouth to speak but he shakes his head. "Let's talk about something else. Like, what do you want to do when you graduate?"

I stare at him. "I don't know. Write, I guess. Or just travel. What about you?"

"Hmm. Porn star." We both laugh. "No, no, I'm serious. I really think I could do it."

"You're that good, are you?"

"Well, no. Honestly, no. You'd be disappointed. But I'm thinking gay porn."

I stifle a laugh and roll my eyes.

"But really, you'd be disappointed," he repeats.

"Don't worry. I wasn't thinking about it."

We sink deeper into the bathwater and finish our smoke. He finally drops the steady smirk he's been wearing and lowers his eyes. "I don't think I could ever sleep with you, really. I'd feel like I was corrupting something."

—

There are over 200 million results on Google for what to do when your friends are on drugs. Most have advice like:

Do not enable your friend.

Encourage your friend to find a 12-step program.

Be direct in your approach.

Gather a variety of possible solutions.

Some ask questions like: Has a friend become moody, short-tempered, and hostile? Does he or she seem out of it or spacey? Be sure they have a drug problem before approaching them.

None of this helps me. I know he has a drug problem, and if he wanted my help, he wouldn't bring this up here, now, like this. What he wants is to be heard. He needs to be understood. If he wanted help, I remind myself, he wouldn't come to me. No. Not me.

—

"Life sucks sometimes," I say.

"Tell me about it."

"I've never told anyone this but you know after we stopped hanging out, I spent three days in the woods somewhere off Highway 25 without any food. I told myself I was looking for God, and fuck was I desperate to find him... or her... or it."

"Any manna come out of the ground? Or ravens drop off some lunch?"

"Not even a still, small voice. I mean, *nothing*. I heard nothing."

"Damn."

"Yeah. But I hiked back to my car the next day, and the first thing I saw lying there on my seat was *A Man without a Country*. I flipped it open to the part where Vonnegut's talking about his uncle Alex, who said one of the greatest things I've ever read."

"What's that?"

"I urge you to please notice when you are happy, and exclaim or murmur or think at some point, 'If this isn't nice, I don't know what is.'"

He laughs.

"I just mean to say, I understand if you want to keep doing what you're doing. It's your life, and I know how good it feels to be that numb. I'm like six deep now and preaching to the choir. But that's what it is: numbness. It isn't euphoria, isn't happiness, isn't peace. It's numb. And even though they seem to be few and far between, there are some absolutely perfect life moments where everything clicks. And it's beautiful. And I would take that over numb—at least most days of the week."

He nods. "You need another drink?"

—

We wake up the next morning cuddled up in the backseat of my Toyota. He calls twice the next day and says he wants to move down to Charleston with me.

"I love you brother, but I don't think that'd be good for either of us," I tell him.

I try, over the next months, to call him at least twenty times. His mom answers and says, "I'm sorry, you're who? I don't know where he is."

I look him up on the internet and find more arrests: possession, possession with intent to distribute, shoplifting, $20,000 bail, $45,000 bail, conviction pending.

I also find out that he broke pitching records on his high school baseball team. He was in school on a full ride.

BIOGRAPHIES

Sam Bilheimer drinks three cups of hot chocolate most days and wonders what everyone else sees in coffee. When he's not editing other people's work for literary magazines or blogs, Sam's either yelling at his guitar or attempting to organize words in just the right order. Sam wishes he remembered how to play the clarinet.

Krystal Davidowitz is a Puerto Rican, Jewish, second-degree black belt who studies criminal justice, political science, and English, all with hopes to fight crime when she graduates.

Coe Douglas is an advertising copywriter, occasional music video director, screenwriter, and documentary filmmaker. Because he feels guilty about one of those, he eats mostly plants to offset his karmic debt. Soon he'll be starting an MFA in fiction at the University of Tampa. He probably drinks too much coffee.

Caroline Fraley is a junior at the University of North Florida. She has a one year-old chocolate lab named Trout who sometimes hikes and kayaks with her, even though he runs off in the woods and won't stay in the boat for more than a few minutes at a time. After she graduates, Caroline dreams of going on tour as a roadie and will probably end up homeless.

Raptor Grant is a writer of surrealistic and gothic fiction, focusing on bridging preternatural elements with the fallen human condition. Raptor currently studies at the University of North Florida in Jacksonville. He would one day like to shock the entire world into a story coma.

Jacob Harn is majoring in English and psychology at the University of North Florida. He enjoys surfing and seems to avoid writing what he feels he must, but when he is able, his writing pulls from the water-edged, strange-tongued, lowly places he has been.

Pamela Hnyla has wandered among the brown brick buildings of UNF since 1990, first as a student (BA '95; MA '98) and then as a writing instructor. Two of her stories, "Genesis" and "God Bless the Child," were recently published online. She will vehemently deny any other publications. In her spare time, she is working on a cure for writer's block.

Miguel Mendoza was born with his umbilical cord wrapped around his neck. But he survived, and now he spends his time writing poems and short stories. He wants to be a novelist, and hopes he doesn't starve before his first novel is published.

Alexa Oliveras enjoys wearing sweat pants, drinking wine, and writing. She received her B.A. in English from UNF in 2013. Alexa volunteers with the Douglas Anderson School of the Arts on various student projects and writes for the D.A. Arts magazine. She lives with her husband and book collection in Jacksonville, Florida.

Heather Peters is not to be confused with the erotica novelist, Heather Peters, or the lawyer involved in the Honda small claims incident, Heather Peters. No, this Heather Peters is pretty boring. But, she has been published in the online literary journal deadpaper.org, as well as Yes, They're Real: A Collection of

Nonfiction. And now that you've read this bio (which was a silly thing to do), please feed some ducks.

Meredith Raiford is not a writer. She just edits and plays with words. She once ate nothing but navel oranges for a week. More of her work can be found scrawled in sarcastic cursive in the margins of discarded daily newspapers.

Carl Rosen is a Spicoli look alike who hates anything Spicolian in nature. He is a self-deprecating author who focuses on postmodern themes, especially suicide and depression. The few times he does leave his room, he finds himself in estranged countries, mingling with natives. He is not religious or "spiritual," in any sense of the word, and strongly believes that "god" should be written with a lowercase "g."

Nicole Sundstrom is a 2013 graduate of UNF with a bachelor's degree in English. Ideally, her dream job would regularly involve wine and Pinterest, but she'd settle for a career in publishing. She is the proud mother of one and auntie of seven...cats. Special thanks to Mark Ari, her parents, and her fiancé, Adrian, for their support.

Michaela Tashjian is a writer from Schenectady, New York. "Unraveling" is one of her first published stories, and she thinks that's splendid. After graduating with a B.A. in English from the University of North Florida, she plans to travel the world. In the meantime, she seeks the Lord, studies, and writes, living with a healthy addiction to semi-colons and British spelling.

You can find more of her work in Tiger's Eye Journal, Inkspill Magazine, and The Penwood Review.

Samuel Wampler was born underneath the statue of a goat king, and so far has lived his life with purpose. Ironically, some people call him a bearish man.

Phillip Wentirine is an English major and creative writing minor at the University of North Florida. Graduating this year, he plans to teach overseas having been inspired by teaching orphans in China during summer 2012. He is an avid marathon runner and relishes in reality TV in his spare time. One day he hopes to make it on *Survivor*. He most likely won't win, but he's hopeful his infectious personality, along with the jokes sometimes only he laughs at, will get him to the jury.

Hurley Winkler is an English major at the University of North Florida. She eats pizza and knits in her apartment in Neptune Beach, Florida.

MARK ARI
With our deepest gratitude.

Without Mark Ari, not only would my piece not be in this collection, but this collection would not be in your hands. His encouragement has allowed me to challenge my own literary boundaries and birth stories I never thought possible to write. The raw encouragement and pure enthusiasm he has for his students is beyond anything I could have ever hoped for in the four workshops I've had with him. He is quite possibly the most genuine and kind soul I have ever met and will ever meet—no, without a doubt, he is. Without Ari, my career as a writer would be ambiguous.

Ari, you are loved more than you could ever possibly know, clichés and all.

—*Phillip Wentirine*

Great professors are made from great human beings. Mark Ari is both. From my first workshop last semester to now, he's taught me to believe in my writing—encouraging me to pursue it in spite of my self-doubt. He always knows just how to find the heart of a story and how to push it in the direction of becoming what it wants to be. Even in the short time I've known him, Ari has changed the way that I think about crafting words. He's made me love the sentence. But more importantly, through his honesty and through his love for his students, he's given us all a beautiful role model for life outside the classroom as well.

—*Caroline Fraley*

Mark Ari's reputation is legendary. I first heard of his genius four years ago when I started taking creative writing courses. But by some horrible stroke of luck it was not until recently that I've had the wonderful opportunity to absorb some of his magic. I now understand why his students always spoke so well of him. Mark Ari approaches his students' creativity with encouragement, understanding, and a complete willingness to be immersed in their stories.

A writer's life is hard enough, but thankfully, writers have Mark Ari.

—Miguel Mendoza

It's hard to describe the appreciation that I have for Mark Ari, but I'm going to try. He has been the greatest and most influential professor I've had in my four years at UNF. Without him, I wouldn't have had the opportunity to be in something as amazing as this. Ari has given me confidence in my writing and in myself as a writer. His passion for writing is infectious, and he genuinely cares about each and every one of his students. Being in his classes has been an honor.

—Krystal Davidowitz

I know of no kindness like the kindness of strangers, and of no stranger kinder than Mark Ari. In a rather innocuous Facebook post between acquaintances, this stranger, Ari, reached out to my strange dream and unknowingly refueled it as it was reaching empty. I am forever indebted.

—Meredith Raiford

Mark Ari once told me, "If you're not making mistakes, you're not a good writer." In addition to telling me that, he's worked through those mistakes in my writing with me. I've never had someone in my life so dedicated to helping me with my work. I am happy to call Ari a trustworthy friend.

—Hurley Winkler

Mark Ari is the most inspirational teacher and person I've had the pleasure of meeting during my college career. He's pushed me to become a better writer, a more open and adventurous person, and he's inspired me to believe in my writing. He encourages everyone of all backgrounds and walks of life to stand up and let their voices be heard because they matter, and that's what makes him an outstanding teacher and person. My biggest regret of my college career (including freshman year, and that says a lot!) is not having taken Ari sooner. He's changed the way I write, the way I think, and the person I've become, and I can never thank him enough.

—Nicole Sundstrom

Mark Ari has had a tremendous impact on my writing, not only as a craft or an art form, but as a lifestyle. He has challenged me more than any earthly mentor I have ever had, and has trained my eyes to see beyond the boundaries of what is true, and what is less than true. Because of the depth of his concern and kindness for his students and for me, I hesitate to call him "professor." I prefer to call him friend.

—Michaela Tashjian

You'll hear people say they had the greatest teacher ever (and to quote Ari, "If you haven't, it's coming."), but the fact that this book is in your hands proves them wrong. I heard a student joke once that he'd majored in Ari, I've witnessed the glory that is the Rubber Chicken Award, and I've felt the delight in having written something that made Ari proud, made him chuckle, made him say, "Hey, you ought to get that published." Ari has given me more opportunities than any other professor I've had the pleasure of meeting, and has been the most selfless person I believe I've ever known. He'd buy you a beer if you drank, talk books until the sun turned cold, and hug you if you needed one.

—*Heather Peters*

I was floundering and unsure where I wanted my life to go. I found myself in a class with Ari, and he helped me to believe in my own talent and remember my love of writing. Mark Ari cares deeply about many things, most importantly people. This quality is the best one a person can have. He is not selfish with his talents but encourages and inspires talent in others as well.

—*Alexa Oliveras*

Ari is inspiring. Don't take my word for it. Read everything that everyone else has written. In a world rather hostile to creative endeavors, he makes rooms full of passionate writers understand that what they are doing is important and necessary. And *that* is important and necessary.

—*Pamela Hnyla*

Mark Ari is an incredibly passionate teacher who inspires within his students the drive to reach their full creative potential. Ask anyone who has had him, and they'll tell you the same thing. Having even just a single iota of Ari in their lives has made them all the better. I know it's true for me, and I've seen it with others. I'm so grateful for everything Ari has done for me.

—*Raptor Grant*

Ari's voice inflects, excites, and gives his words the arc of a good story. His hands start waving, and his hair falls over his forehead in that Ari-esque way. Then he looks up into the eyes of those attentively listening, and he brushes his hair back into place—and you realize, he has just danced through those dense recesses of the brain and has returned with the invaluable insights of a wise man who navigates the world with curiosity and passion. When he reads a piece, his voice becomes a conduit through which writing is illuminated. Ari once said, "I'm not a man of absolutes." This will forever resonate with me. Not only did it give me a way to identify my own tendency toward uncertainty, but it attracted me to language all the more. The examples of Ari's profound influence go on and on. Until you know him yourself, you'll just have to trust he's a mentor in compassion, he seems to have an inborn knowledge of the human condition, and that he's a teacher's teacher. He is an example of how to approach your life. He is an absolute treasure.

—*Jacob Harn*

The Friday before I was set to meet up with Ari for the first time to have coffee, I met him accidentally at an event for the late poet Alan Justiss at the Karpeles Manuscript Museum. Ari was immediately kind, engaged, and thrilled to bump into me a few days early. I mostly remember his iconic hat, perfectly

Whitman-like on his head. In short time, our recurring coffee-chats led to a giant stack of new books to read and a fantastic new internship program created between my agency, St. John & Partners, and UNF, bringing two talented creative writing students to the SJ&P creative department. I also met a kindred spirit and made a friend I'll have for the rest of my life. Ari is a fantastic human being. As a writer, teacher, and mentor, he's a constant reminder of what passion and love of one's art can look like.

—*Coe Douglas*

Some people just shake your hand and barely acknowledge your existence, and this is something far more common than not, but then you meet someone like Ari, whose handshake requires two hands—it starts with the typical hand to hand interlace, but then his off hand comes around and fastens on your shoulder. The second hand cements the embrace and reassures you that you're going to be okay, whether you're on the brink of peril or not. What's most testimonial to his character is that his handshake isn't reserved for a select few, it's how he greets any stranger.

—*Carl Rosen*

I've not met a person on Earth more passionate than Ari, and I don't believe I ever will.

—*Sam Bilheimer*

Made in the USA
Charleston, SC
08 May 2016